THE GOOD POETIC MOTHER

THE GOOD POETIC MOTHER
A DAUGHTER'S MEMOIR

Irene Hoge Smith

International Psychoanalytic Books (IPBooks)
New York • http://www.IPBooks.net

Published by International Psychoanalytic Books (IPBooks)
Queens, NY
Online at www.IPBooks.net

Copyright © 2021 Irene Smith Landsman, PhD

All rights reserved. No part of this publication may be reproduced, stored in a retrieval system, or transmitted in any form or by any means, electronic, mechanical, photocopying, recording or otherwise, without the prior written permission from the publisher.

Front cover design by Kathy Kovacic
Book design and formatting services by Noel S. Morado

ISBN: 978-1-949093-87-2

*With love and gratitude to my husband, Ron,
and infinite admiration and affection for my children,
Patrick and EJ.*

*In memory of my mother,
Frances Dean Smith (francEyE) 1922–2009.*

...but finally when I think of her
life
and compare it to other lives
more dazzling, original
and beautiful
I realize that she has hurt fewer
people than anybody I know....
and if you look at it
like that,
well,
she has created a better world
she has won.
Frances, this poem is for
you.
—Charles Bukowski, "One For Old Snaggle-tooth"

I rest as the day warms, hear
through closed windows the faint repeated call
of the fog horn, three miles away. It warns off
sailors but I don't know who those sailors are,
and it warns me: You are not in charge. Your
children can be taken from you,
your life ended over and over
before it is over. Listen,
it says: A voice. That's
all you have.

—francEyE, "Call"

CONTENTS

AUTHOR'S NOTE xi
PREFACE xiii
PANDORA'S BOX (WASHINGTON, 2009) 1
GOODNIGHT IRENE (WASHINGTON, 2017) 10
ALREADY BROKEN (WASHINGTON, 1950) 14
RIVERSIDE (CALIFORNIA, 1951 to 1954) 17
LOST AND FOUND (MICHIGAN, 1955) 30
PICKET LINE (MICHIGAN, 1956) 33
FAMILY CAMP (WISCONSIN, 1957) 35
SCAPEGOAT (MICHIGAN, 1957) 40
ANXIOUS ATTACHMENT (MICHIGAN, 1960) 45
FATHER'S DAY (MICHIGAN, 1961) 53
ROUND ONE (WASHINGTON, 1961) 57
ROUND TWO (MICHIGAN, 1962) 70
FOSTER CHILD (MICHIGAN, 1962) 79
SUNDAY SCHOOL (MICHIGAN, 1962) 89
SHE'S HAD IT (MICHIGAN, 1962) 93
GOODBYE TO ALL THAT (MICHIGAN, 1962) 100
UP ON THE ROOF (WASHINGTON, 1963) 105
DERELICTION OF DUTY (WASHINGTON, 1963) 109

DON'T THINK (NEW YORK, 1963) 120
SICK DAY (NEW YORK, 1964) 127
MEET YOUR SISTER (WASHINGTON, 1965) 138
KEEPSAKES (WASHINGTON, 1965) 142
MANIFESTO (WASHINGTON, 1965) 148
MARCH ON WASHINGTON (WASHINGTON, 1965) 158
FAILURE TO LAUNCH (TEXAS, 1967) 164
TRANSCRIPT OF RECORD (WASHINGTON, 1968) 172
RUNAWAY MOTHER (CALIFORNIA, 1981) 183
THE PLEASURE OF YOUR COMPANY (WASHINGTON, 1988) 192
NOTHING TO SAY (WASHINGTON, 1984, 1994, 2000, 2004) 200
GRANDMA STORIES (CALIFORNIA, 2007) 211
NOT UNTRUE AND NOT UNKIND (CALIFORNIA, 2009) 223
ACKNOWLEDGMENTS 231
PERMISSIONS 233

AUTHOR'S NOTE

This is a work of memoir. It represents events as best I can remember them, and dialogue has been recreated based on actual exchanges that I recall. My own memories have been supplemented by other invaluable resources—letters from my mother, a late-life interview with her, and a journal discovered after her death. A few names have been changed.

Conventions for culturally-sensitive terminology regarding race change over time, and I have tried to be respectful of evolving standards. In passages describing what I was taught as a child in the 1950s, I use the terms "colored" and "Negro." In passages set in the 1960s and later I capitalize "Black," and in keeping with some current guidelines I do the same for "White."

PREFACE

> "To Irene Smith — of the good poetic mother.
> Yrs., Charles Bukowski, 8-3-63"

I was fifteen when I received a signed copy of the underground poet's breakout book, *It Catches My Heart in Its Hands*. Bukowski's title comes from a Robinson Jeffers poem, and mine comes from this inscription, written to me more than half a century ago.

I never met Bukowski, and was not able to appreciate his poems at the time, but this collection remains one of the most physically beautiful volumes I've ever owned. The publisher's note about the materials and methods of its creation is almost a poem itself: "777 copies of this book were printed by the editors of Loujon Press, one page at a time, handfed with 12-point Garamond Old Style for the poems, 18-point Pabst O.S. for the titles—to an ancient 8 by 12 Chandler & Price letterpress; on Linweave Spectra paper throughout, 310 lb. for the cover, 160 lb. for the jacket, 75 lb. for the text, in shades of white, winestone, saffron, bayberry, peacock, ivory, bittersweet, gobelin & tobasco."

I almost threw it out.

My poet mother had been gone almost a year when this perplexing gift arrived. After a bad marriage and an even worse divorce, my fa-

THE GOOD POETIC MOTHER

ther had the deeds to two houses, the family car, and custody of their four daughters. She was, as she said later, "loose on my own, a failure at motherhood," and had to find a new life. Leaving the East Coast behind forever, she fled to California, where she met the outsider poet whose writings she'd already read and admired.

She first mentioned someone called "Charles" in a letter from Los Angeles. "I have been up at C's since Sunday." She enclosed a poem about gardens, children, and death, "which I recited to him in a flush of self-esteem in between some poems of his that he was reading to me. Charles said it was good—wow!"

She never referred to him as "Charles" again—Henry Charles Bukowski was "Hank" to his friends—but even without knowing who this man was, I resented him. For another year I would hold on to a faint hope that my mother might eventually return, but when she and Bukowski had their own daughter, I gave up. Like a spurned lover, I turned against her, against him, and probably even against the blameless little baby.

That resentment was unsurprising. Still too much a child to care anything about the happiness of a parent, I joined my father in a dismissive attitude toward my mother and her projects. I came into adulthood doing my best to ignore her existence.

A child who has been left might seem to be the person least able to make sense of her mother's experience, but at the same time she may be precisely the one most compelled to do so. Several years ago, when I began the New Directions program at the Washington Center for Psychoanalysis, one of our group leaders invited the new students to reflect on what brought us to the three-year writing course. With some reluctance, I admitted that I had a complicated relationship to writing and to writers. My mother, I explained, was a poet. That might have been all right, but she left the family when I was young, ran

AUTHOR'S NOTE

away to California, lived with Charles Bukowski, and had his child. At some level I feared writing had the dark power to make a person leave those who loved and needed her most, and quite possibly enter a life of incomprehensible strangeness.

The group leader, a poet herself, listened thoughtfully. "You know," she finally said, "you may have to write about your mother in order to write about anything else."

Friends and fellow writers often find it difficult to see beyond the fact of my mother's leaving. Others, perhaps pained by the sad litany of loss, wonder if they should encourage me to forgive her. But whatever this book is about, it is not about the kind of forgiveness so often preached as a panacea, a wishful assertion that someone who has been hurt will be miraculously freed by the simple decision to forgive.

Forgiveness is both more complicated than that, and much more simple. Most religions have some teachings regarding forgiveness, and they are fundamentally quite similar. In order to forgive, we must *give up* something. Most simply, we have to relinquish the wish for revenge, retaliation, or recompense. In that regard I feel on relatively solid ground—I don't recall ever trying to make my mother suffer, or even wishing that she would. I wanted to tell my own story, but I didn't do it to hurt her or anyone else.

Forgiveness does not guarantee reconciliation, but it does require acknowledging the humanity of the person in question. I might easily have written my mother as a caricature—a foolish, self-involved woman, more attached to her writing and political beliefs than to her children, whose abandonment of those children defined her. I knew from the perspective of writing, emotional health, and maybe even the good of my soul, whatever that might be, how important it was not to fall into that trap.

Finally, to forgive someone does not mean to forget what has happened, but to be able to wish the other well despite our own pain. My mother is gone now, but I respect her lifelong dedication to poetry, and am glad that she felt loved by the one daughter she was able to mother. I'm sorry not to have been a beneficiary of that late-developed capacity, but if it were up to me I'd want their relationship to have existed rather than not. I'm relieved to know that she died free of pain and fear, and that she was not wracked by guilt. I hope that, if she is somewhere now, she is at peace.

For our own sake, and perhaps for the sake of the world, we are enjoined to give up thoughts of revenge, relinquish enduring resentment, grant to the other person their own essential worth, and practice compassion to them and to ourselves.

We are not required to write a book about them. I did that for myself.

PANDORA'S BOX (WASHINGTON, 2009)

"Are you sure you want all this?" My sister Sara was at my front door, holding a battered cardboard carton, her smile apologetic. "I don't know how much of a gift it's going to be."

She had called me a week before to say our stepmother had something for us, some writings of our mother's. What they were, where they'd come from—Sara didn't know any of that.

Our mother had been dead for three months, but in truth, we had lost her a long time before. After an impetuous decision to divorce and a protracted wrangle over who was going to have to take care of us, our mother had gotten the short end of a bad stick in the early 1960s. In the end, she was officially an unfit mother, and our father looked like a hero to the outside world for taking in four girls, aged four to sixteen. My sisters and I left Michigan to join him in Washington, D.C., our mother fled to California, and we never lived with her again.

Sara is six years younger than I; the middle two of four sisters, we were fifty-four and sixty that summer. Our baby sister Ruthie had

THE GOOD POETIC MOTHER

died in her forties, and the oldest, Patti, had long since cut off all contact with the family. There were just the two of us left.

I took the carton from Sara's hands and was immediately surprised by its weight. "Wow—feels like bricks." I set the box on the floor, careful to bend my knees. Sara wiped her hands on her pink sweatshirt.

"No bricks, just paper. Lots and lots and lots of paper."

Sara followed me back to the kitchen, where I set the cardboard container on the table and we regarded it with trepidation. Corrugated cardboard, ten by seven by thirteen inches, "Georgia" and "49" and "RH 2401" written on top in bold black marker.

"That carton looks like something Daddy would have brought home from his office—maybe when he worked for that congressman?" Sara turned the carton and pointed to crooked penciled letters on the side, reading "FD SMITH stuff."

"What do you make of this? It doesn't look like his handwriting to me."

I had set out an assortment of tea bags and we waited for the water to boil, letting the still-hot soda bread cool enough to slice. I took two green ceramic mugs from the cupboard, and we inhaled the inviting warm smell of sugar, currents and caraway seed. "Good idea," Sara grinned. "It's probably too early to open a bottle of wine." I laughed, and realized I'd been frowning since I opened the front door.

We settled ourselves at the table, and over the next hour we talked about our mother, her funeral, and whether the contents of this mysterious box were likely to shed any light on our understanding of her. Sara had glanced at some of the papers but couldn't really characterize the collection. "That's why I hoped you'd take it, at least for a while. It's kind of unsettling."

PANDORA'S BOX (WASHINGTON, 2009)

All we knew for sure is that this box had been in our father's possession from the time our mother left at the end of 1962 until his death in 2000. It didn't seem that the box had ever been opened, and we didn't know if our stepmother had always known of it, or had only recently discovered it. But it was ours now.

I am a clinical psychologist, and I had just finished the second year of a three-year writing program at my local psychoanalytic institute. I'd worked through my resistance to being a writer like my mother (a poet who only came into her own creative life after she left), and was reluctantly beginning to recognize that the book I needed to write would be about her. I had a writing corner next to two south-facing windows in a large upstairs bedroom, a space that represented my intention to maintain a practice of writing, to keep it going through the times when I felt I had nothing to say or that what I had to say no one would want to read. A set of shelves gave me a third wall and sixteen square cubbies, more than enough space for a growing collection of craft books, essay collections, and folders of my own writing.

After Sara left me with what I'd started calling just "The Box," I found myself reluctant to bring it into this sanctuary. It had been hard enough to retrieve my mother's old letters from a file drawer where I'd tried to forget them for too many years. Those letters were now in a new sage-green cardboard box, with a small metal label holder, as if a nicer container might make the contents more manageable. Months after my mother died, I was more depressed than I liked to admit, and it took a lot of organization to keep myself together.

THE GOOD POETIC MOTHER

While less than a cubic foot in volume, the package, filled with folders and loose sheets of typing paper, strained my hands and forearms as I carried it upstairs. I lowered the carton into yet another color-coordinated storage box, and put that in one of my cubbies, where it would stay for several weeks before I felt up to actually opening it, unpacking the contents, and trying to make sense of what my mother left behind.

When I did return to The Box, I started at the top, examining each envelope and typescript individually. I wouldn't try to read anything, not yet, just remove items one at a time, stacking them with care, as if preserving the original order—like an archeologist excavating an ancient dig—might turn out to be crucial to understanding this history. I jotted down notes for each unearthed item as I brought it up into daylight.

1. A letter to the editor of the *Ann Arbor News*, dated January 22, 1960: "Tonight's Reader's Viewpoint asks a couple of leading questions which invite comment…."

2. A six-line poem, recounting a story I remembered my mother telling:

> *AUTOBIOGRAPHY*
> *Infants are like apes,*
> *my father said;*
> *Look at her swing.*
> *I was two days old. I gripped*
> *the chandelier,*
> *while he laughed to see his seed on the ceiling screaming.*
> *Frances Dean Smith*

3. A red folder, containing numerous sheets of paper with children's drawings, tic-tac-toe games, and doodles.

4. A sheaf of carbon copy pages—in Cyrillic type. I remembered that my mother had studied Russian when we lived in Ann Arbor, before she and my father split up. I couldn't imagine what this document was, but felt relieved that these twenty pages, at least, were ones I wouldn't have to try to understand.

5. A black faux-leather springback binder, containing a collection of my mother's poems—ninety-three separate works organized by form (sonnets, villanelles, triolets, and so on). I recognized "Snowdream," about snowshoe rabbits and blood on snow, which I knew had been published in the *Saturday Review* before I was born. The collection was inscribed "To Smitty, with love—and, yes, some thought. From Fran." Smitty was my mother's nickname for my paternal grandmother, Madeleine Tyler Smith. Our father had called her "Nanine," my sisters and I called her "Nanny," and she was the best mother any of us would ever have.

6. A spiral-bound pocket notebook with an orange cover. There were seventy-seven lined sheets in this notebook, covered on both sides with closely-written ballpoint script. The first page read: "Mrs. W. Smith, 853 Third Street, S.W., Washington 24, D.C.," followed by a list:

> *What do you feel?*
> *What do you want?*
> *What do you do about it?*
> *I exist. I experience.*
> *I'm important.*

THE GOOD POETIC MOTHER

7. A seven-by-ten-inch composition book, with "August 10, 1961–August 22, 1961" written on the black-and-white marbled cover. The first of ninety-six pages began in the middle of a sentence. Were there some pages missing? I wasn't sure the sentence would have made sense even if had been complete.

> —*these red faces with their sharp noses. It was at the time I dreamed it nearly unbearable. It was all I could do to describe the drama to Dr. Kleinerman, I could not discuss it.*

(Dr. Kleinerman, I ascertained eventually, had been a Washington psychiatrist my mother consulted in the early years of her marriage.)

I eventually abandoned the archeological approach, sorted the contents by category, arranged a dozen piles on the floor of my writing nook, and was at least able to summarize what I had:

Ten letters to the editor and eight more (also contentious) to individuals; thirteen stories and eight essays; twenty-two pieces for a newspaper column called *Fran Thinks;* fifty-two drawings, paintings, and paper constructions made by children; five photographs; three church bulletins; three song sheets; a National Gallery of Art handout describing Salvador Dali's *The Sacrament of the Last Supper*; one hundred sixty-three poems, two personal journals, and a novel.

Almost a thousand separate pieces of paper.

The afternoon passed quickly, and when I looked out the window I saw scores of crows flying toward and over the house in a darkening sky, cawing companionably. Every morning they flew out together, over my neighborhood to farms and fields to the south. At sunset they returned to their roost, high in stands of tulip poplar and oak a mile north. I found comfort in their familiar routine, seeing them venture forth in the company of their kind, always knowing where to find home. Their calls reminded me that I had a safe home, too, and that it was time to make dinner. I put my mother's box back in the larger box and set it back on the shelf, and, when my husband let himself in the back door, I was in the kitchen, finishing a tomato sauce fragrant with oregano and basil, feeling better than I had all day.

"How did it go"? He knew I was determined to learn everything I could from this unexpected cache of my mother's words and that I often found the process intolerable.

"It's like the box is radioactive—each thing I read is confusing and crazy, and I swear whatever she had, it's contagious."

I didn't see patients on Fridays, reserving that time for writing, and since I finally recognized that I was writing a book, and that it was going to be about my mother, the project of "The Box" counted as writing research. After my husband left for his office, and I had finished reading the *Washington Post* over an English muffin and my first cup of coffee, and then had a second cup of coffee and read parts of the paper I usually skip, I tried to be ready to work. If I didn't spend too long in any one stretch reading and trying to understand these items and writings, the task seemed like something that might eventually be finished.

I picked up the composition book. After nine pages of hard-to-follow rambling, I found a date, "August 12," and these lines:

THE GOOD POETIC MOTHER

Mother was a snob—the wrong kind of snob! Any kind of snob is wrong, since the word means a person who feels superior to other people for false reasons. The thing is to know yourself and know what kind of people you like and what kind of people like you. Or what people you like and what people like you, that's better, and to know that everybody wants to be liked and

This, like the small orange notebook, was a diary, and I realized that the two journals overlapped, both having entries from mid-August to early September, 1961. I concluded that she had used the smaller orange pad when she was out and about, and the composition book when she was at home, wherever that was. It was going to be a job to try to correlate them.

Somewhere in the middle of the stack of papers was a folder labeled "Novel," containing an inch-thick manuscript. Even less interested in her fiction than her polemics, I had put the folder aside at least twice, without reading any of it, and here is where I had to face an uncomfortable truth. Despite a conscious wish to understand my mother, once I began sifting through her writings I could not maintain interest in what she was thinking and doing unless I thought it might have something to do with *me*. That had been true since the first letter I received from her in 1963—I was fourteen, she'd been gone for six months, and in that letter, as in the ones I received over the years, and now in these pages of poetry and prose, I was seeking not a story, but a mother. Did she think about me? Care about me? Had I been there? And since in all of her writings there was almost no evidence of a mother-daughter relationship, I found it harder to assimilate much of what I did find.

Since I hadn't been able to make much sense of her two journal notebooks, I decided to see what, if anything, I might glean from the novel. The prose was organized in sections, from a few lines to several pages in length, each headed with a date. It took several minutes before I realized, with a mix of fascination and dread, that what I was holding was not a novel at all, but her own story. She had transcribed her journals, and those more than two hundred typewritten pages narrated the weeks from April through August. The final week duplicated entries in the two notebooks, which in turn continued to September 4, 1961. Taken together, these writings contained an almost-daily record of what had been on her mind over the course of the five months when my parents' marriage came apart.

GOODNIGHT IRENE (WASHINGTON, 2017)

"I'll have a Grande skim latte, please."

The barista had a broad grin, close-cropped dark hair, and a wisp of goatee. He was not as old as my youngest child. "Can I have a name for the order?"

"Irene," I said. Someone turned on the espresso machine.

"Eileen?"

"No, Irene, with an R." *I suppose I could just let it be Eileen*, I thought, not for the first time.

He marked the cup, still smiling.

"Tell me," I asked him. "if I had said 'Irene, like the song,' would that mean anything to you?"

"I'm afraid not." Apologetic, he looked down at the cash drawer.

"How about if I said, 'like the hurricane?'"

"Oh, yeah," he laughed.

A few summers back, that hurricane was bad enough that the name has been retired. No more Katrina, no more Sandy, no more Irene.

GOODNIGHT IRENE (WASHINGTON, 2017)

Goodnight Irene, goodnight Irene
I'll see you in my dreams

I was two the year the Weavers' hit single topped the charts for six months, and as far back as I can remember adults would start singing to me when they heard my name. I didn't know why they thought it was so funny, or how they could always think they were the first ones to make the connection. As much as I craved attention, I was painfully self-conscious—I'd duck my head and back out of the room, protesting, "I hate that song!"

I asked your mother for you
She told me you was too young
I wish to the Lord I never seen your face
I'm sorry you ever was born

The song made me special, for a while and to some people, and I'm wistful now that it's mostly forgotten. But it was always complicated. My mother named me not for the popular and sweet Weaver's version, but for the original, a dark and hopeless ballad by the blues singer Lead Belly. The melody is lovely, but the words tell a story of anger and despair. It was the first song I ever heard, and sometimes I can almost remember the crib, a dim room and my mother singing.

I love Irene, God knows I do
I'll love her till the sea runs dry
And if Irene turns her back on me
I'm gonna take morphine and die.

THE GOOD POETIC MOTHER

She had a pretty voice, but didn't care much for pretty songs. Of all the ballads in *The Fireside Book of Folksongs* she was drawn most to those with themes of dissolution and destruction. She thought we should know not just the words, but what they meant. Lily Marlene, underneath the lamppost, was a prostitute. Willie the Weeper was addicted to cocaine. Foggy, foggy dew means whiskey, and Joe Hill was framed. She sang all the verses of "Goodnight Irene."

> *Stop rambling, stop your gambling*
> *Stop stayin' out late at night*
> *Go home to your wife and your family*
> *Stay home by the fireside bright.*

Her father, the brilliant young grandpa I never knew, might have been the last person she really loved. He fell ill when she was six years old, and for almost two years she was told he'd get well and come home. But she never saw him again, never got over it, and never forgave her mother for lying to her.

> *Sometimes I live in the country*
> *Sometimes I live in town*
> *Sometimes I take a great notion*
> *To jump in the river and drown.*

My mother, her little sister, and their mother were poor relations in her grandfather's big house, where she couldn't be friends with the milkman's boy (because it wouldn't do) or bring her friend Molly home to play (because the Irish will steal). She gave up hoping that anyone would ever love her again, and was thirteen years old the first time she tried to kill herself. She tied a rope around her neck and jumped from her grandfather's apple tree. The rope was rotten, it broke, and she wept.

> *Goodnight Irene, goodnight Irene*
> *I'll see you in my dreams*

She didn't warn me, probably because it wasn't really a plan, just the thing that had to happen when all other options had been lost or destroyed. She left when I was fourteen, and I didn't see it coming any more than she'd believed her father would really die.

> *She caused me to weep, she caused me to moan*
> *She caused me to leave my home*
> *And the very last words I ever heard her say,*
> *was, please sing me one more song.*

ALREADY BROKEN (WASHINGTON, 1950)

My big sister had been right there, and then she wasn't, and outside, down on the sidewalk, someone was screaming. The round second-story room was filled with sunlight, and a warm breeze came from the high curved windows. Where was she? Grownups were shouting and I was scared and ashamed and I pulled back from the window. I'd done something wrong but I didn't know what it was.

This is my first memory. I was two and Patti was four and we lived with our parents in our grandmother's brick row house in the Capitol Hill neighborhood of Washington, D.C. Nanny had left her bullying husband behind in Arizona when Patti was born, come East to help with the baby, and never left Washington again. We lived with her for the first two years of my life.

This is the story about Patti and the window that I grew up believing: she and I had been up before the grownups and maybe looking for mischief. We'd been playing tag and I was the one chasing and Patti was the one running and she was going too fast and ran into the window screen. The screen fell out and she did, too, landing on the sidewalk two stories down, just missing a spiked iron fence. Our father ran downstairs to see what happened, then back upstairs to get his car keys, and by the time he got back to the sidewalk somebody else had taken Patti to the hospital. She broke an arm and a leg.

My own memory of the actual event consists only of the image of that sunny room, my sister's presence and absence, shouting, and a feeling of fear or shame or both. My next recollection is of a month or so later, by which time we'd left Nanny's house and moved to Annapolis, Maryland, where our father taught for a year. I remember Patti "dressed in a cast," having to be helped up and down, perhaps not being much fun.

We told the story about Patti and the window many times as we grew up, whenever kids were comparing stories about scars and accidents. It always had the parts about playing tag and a window screen, and our father running up and down stairs. Sometimes she missed the fence by feet, sometimes by inches, but this version was the one we could tell without our father getting angry or our mother starting to cry.

After our parents split up and our mother left, Patti ran away from home. She was seventeen, I was fourteen, and we never lived together again. We had almost no relationship, infrequent contact, and few opportunities to review old stories. I'm not sure, now, when we had the telephone conversation in which she had something very different to say about how she went out that window at four.

We hadn't been playing tag, Patti said, but we had been naughty—playing dress-up, putting on brand-new dresses we'd been told not to touch because they were for someone's wedding. Listening to her, I had an unbidden image; not quite a memory. Brushed nylon, smocking, pastels—maybe pink and mint green. I seemed to remember the irresistible pull of something forbidden. Our father was the one who caught us, she said, and he had become enraged. "My arm was already broken when I went out the window," she told me.

    She mentioned a therapist and hospital records and the fact that it had been her right arm but her left leg that were broken, and how she had recovered or reconstructed her own memory of what happened that day. She believed our father had pushed, or maybe even thrown, her out the window. Finally, she told me that, as an adult, she had confronted our father with what she remembered. His response, she said, was, "Well, the statute of limitations has run out on that."

RIVERSIDE (CALIFORNIA, 1951 to 1954)

I was not quite three when we moved to California and a treeless village of Quonset huts on a former military base in Riverside. Both of our parents had been in the Army (they met on a Signal Corps base near Washington) and the Quonsets provided temporary housing for veterans and their families. We lived on a dusty alley called Callahan Court.

No trace of the alley or the Quonsets remains, but there are still a few things that I remember about Callahan Court:

I remember the shy Japanese woman who had no children of her own, didn't speak English, but smiled at us and made sticky rice eggs. The rice was sweet and not what I expected; I didn't like it but was sorry to make her sad. Mama said she was a war bride. I remember the icebox and the ice man, the pale green water tank and the Culligan man, and I remember the old lady who told us not to touch the gardenias next to her stoop because the glossy white blossoms would turn brown. Maybe she was somebody's grandmother, I thought, like my Nanny back in Washington—whom I could still remember, just a little.

Less than a year after our arrival in Riverside, Mama and I took the train back to Washington.

I couldn't go back and I was afraid to keep going. Mama and I had to get from one train car to the next one and it was too loud and too shaky and I could see the ground rushing by right under my feet. How did Mama know I wouldn't slip between the edge of the sliding metal floor and the banging sides? She reminded me that I was nearly four and that I wasn't really scared. She wasn't mad at me yet but I could tell she wasn't changing her mind. We were going to visit Nanny. Mama told me I remembered Nanny and would be glad to see her but I didn't really remember her anymore. I wanted to know where my sister was and why Daddy wasn't coming with us, but Mama would only answer maybe two or three questions before she snapped at me or started to cry.

This is another story I grew up believing: that when I was four I got to go with my mother on a train all the way from California to Washington, that we were visiting my grandmother, and that it was just me and Mama because my big sister didn't get to go. The truth was more complicated and much darker, as my mother recounted decades later. She and my father had been fighting; he objected to her housekeeping, and she was unhappy, finding California brown and dead and missing the East where she'd grown up. One day she decided she just had to leave, and told him so.

"Well, you're not taking my babies!" he shouted.

She hadn't expected that. Stunned into acquiescence by her husband's anger (not for the first or last time) she agreed that my six-year-old sister could stay with him in California. I never got a clear story of why Patti was left behind (or why I was not), and even in her old age my mother's account remained disjointed. "I just don't know. I knew Patti loved her father and of course he loved her too, and I thought it would be all right."

It wasn't. Not all right for Patti, or for our relationship, and the fact that we don't know each other today may go all the way back to the choice my mother had been forced to make when we were so small.

I remember a big man in a dark suit with gold on his hat who picked me up. Maybe he thought I was too big for Mama to carry, but he didn't know that she wouldn't carry me even if she could, or that she didn't love me when I was scared. Back in the scratchy seats, I was hungry again and Mama gave me another box of raisins and two peanut butter crackers from the cellophane package. I liked the crackers and I liked raisins, but by the third day I didn't like them anymore and Mama didn't want to hear about it. "Don't be stupid. You know you love these. Maybe when you get hungrier you'll like them better." I didn't know how long we'd been on that train and how much longer it was going to be. I didn't want to have to live on raisins and peanut butter crackers forever, was bored looking out the window—at faraway mountains, sometimes a river, the backs of houses—and tired of pretending I remembered somebody called Nanny.

Then we were at Nanny's house and I still didn't remember her but when she kissed me and hugged me she was really soft and smelled nice and I wasn't so shy with her.

THE GOOD POETIC MOTHER

Her house looked like a castle, with a corner tower and tall windows and a spiky black fence. Mama and I slept in the same bed and when I woke up and she wasn't there I sucked my thumb and rubbed the silky edge of the blanket and tried not to cry. One afternoon I found a penny on the floor and wanted to show it to Nanny. Her kitchen was in the basement and the black-and-white checkerboard tiles had been the first thing I thought I remembered when we got there. I was hurrying down the stairs to show Nanny the penny, then tripped and tumbled the last two or three steps to the bottom. I wasn't really hurt but I couldn't find the penny and I couldn't stop crying. Nanny said she'd find me another one, and she held me for a long time. And then I really did remember her.

The train trip to visit Nanny was always one of the things I thought I knew for certain about my own autobiography. Because neither of my parents ever talked about it, the sanitized account of a pleasant visit stayed unchanged in some compartment of my own mind. It was a rare good memory, and it had Nanny in it, and my mother, and it also covered over an earlier and more difficult set of events that I will never ever be able to recall.

When I was born, my mother had been terrified of what a second baby might do to her already-fragile mental equilibrium. She returned to work immediately, and for the first two years of my life it was my grandmother, not my mother, who took care of me. Nanny was a warm woman with a seemingly innate nurturing gift, and I was, according to my mother's later account, very attached to her. I barely knew my parents. "You cried when Nanny wasn't there, or when your father and I wanted to take you to Lincoln Park," my mother said later.

That early connection to my grandmother was a complicated legacy. She was, I think, more capable of maternal attachment than my mother, and, having left her own husband, not compromised by a dysfunctional marriage as my mother so often was. But that early separation from my Nanny-mother, like Patti's later one from her real mother, cast a long shadow across my psychic life.

We weren't "visiting" Nanny, but had moved back in with her, and I learned eventually that our stay in D.C. lasted at least nine months. At some point my sister joined us, and I started to get to know Nanny again and began to forget my father. I have no memory of our return to California, although it may have been another train trip. When I was almost fifty and my mother seventy-five, she wrote to me, "I think of you so often when I am on a train. It's because of the train rides back and forth across the country that we took in 1952. I don't remember much about the trip; I just remember very powerful feelings of joy and despair—joy and delight in you, and despair about my life."

I don't know why we didn't stay in Washington, living with Nanny, going to nursery school and then grade school, our mother continuing to work. She and Nanny were close, and the house had more than enough room for all of us. I assume it was my father's insistence, maybe actual or implied promises, perhaps again the power of him wanting my mother, or, even more spell-binding, needing her. But

THE GOOD POETIC MOTHER

he was changeable, as she recounted later; possessive one moment, rejecting the next. And as it turned out, once my mother brought me and Patti back to California, she and my father separated again almost immediately. He was involved with someone else, not interested in talking with their Unitarian minister about how to make the marriage work better, not interested in talking to my mother about anything at all.

After Callahan Court, Patti and I lived with our mother in three different houses before our father came back, but the only one I remember is the house on Madison Street, where we were when I started school; where, on her own, our mother wasn't managing very well. She often slept through the alarm, unable to organize breakfast and school clothes or to face the day.

Patti said we should leave Mama alone and get our own breakfast, so I pulled a kitchen chair to the counter and climbed up to reach the cornflakes. Patti found a jumper that still fit me and one of her old blouses that was only a little too big. "Is it time to go? Is it time yet?" I couldn't tell time but Patti knew when we had to leave for school and I worried about what would happen if she forgot to look at the clock, or if Mama would wake up in time to come get me at lunch time and whether I could remember how to get home by myself, and what I would do if she was still asleep? Or not there?

I know our mother had some better periods. She held down a part-time job at a local hospital, and I can remember her baking brownies once, using walnuts Patti and I collected from our yard. And I remember the day we came home after dark and saw orange lights flickering across the far end of Madison Street.

RIVERSIDE (CALIFORNIA, 1951 TO 1954)

A forest fire was burning on the ridge of Mount Baldy, and the flames looked like Christmas lights strung across the road. "Would you look at that!" Mama grinned at us. "Yes, it does look like Christmas." It was pretty, but I was scared, too, even though Mama reminded us that Mount Baldy was an hour away and said the firefighters would put the fire out soon and not to be silly. I couldn't fall asleep that night thinking about the fire coming closer and wondering how Mama knew it wouldn't get to us before morning. And then it *was* morning and for once Mama was up and when we all went outside I couldn't see the fire anymore.

"Oh, it's still burning, it's just that you can't see it in daylight." Mama was barefoot in her flannel bathrobe, squinting northward toward the mountains. The air was smoky, other grownups were outside on the sidewalk talking in serious voices, and I couldn't stop asking questions. "How far away is it exactly? How fast does fire spread? What about the animals who live in the forest? Where will the squirrels and chipmunks go?" Mama said the animals could run away from the fire and probably they already had. Her distracted frown didn't keep me from carrying on with my anxious questions.

"Run where? Will they come down the mountain? Even the bears? What about the bears? What if the bears come down to Madison Street and eat us up?" Mama was out of patience. It was silly to think the fire would get anywhere near us and she didn't want any more questions. She said even the other grownups were making a big deal out of nothing.

I knew already that Mama didn't like it when I was afraid. She wasn't afraid of anything in the outdoors. She loved camping and driving up into the mountains, and reminded us that she got the best-all-around-camper medal when she was a girl. We could only go to the mountains now when Daddy was with us, because he had the

THE GOOD POETIC MOTHER

car. But if he did come and we went for a drive usually they weren't yelling and that might be a good day.

Our father's visits, before he finally moved back in with us, were exciting and alarming. His mood determined the emotional tenor of our lives, and I remember that when he was at the Madison Street house everything we did was organized around what we thought he wanted.

"I'll bet you'd like to take Daddy's juice to him, wouldn't you? He'd like that." Daddy had stayed the night, and Mama was not only awake but had combed her hair and put on a pretty blue gathered skirt and a clean white blouse. I did want to be the one to bring him his juice, because then he might notice me and maybe he'd say I was a good girl, but the orange juice was almost up to the top of the glass.

"Be careful now. Walk slowly." I did walk carefully and slowly, into the living room and closer and closer to where Daddy sat frowning at the newspaper unfolded in front of him, his long legs, in khaki weekend slacks, resting on a footstool. He didn't look up as I crept closer, but then all of a sudden he shook the newspaper with a snap, and I jumped, and the juice was all over me and all over the floor, and now I was stupid, stupid, stupid.

"What the hell do you think you're doing, sneaking around like that? Look at this goddamned mess! Can't you do anything right?" I ran to Mama and she said not to worry but go outside and not bother Daddy. I didn't want to be near him anyway. I was mad at myself but mad at him, too. I somehow knew he had snapped the newspaper on purpose, to make me spill the juice and give him an excuse to yell at me.

At dinner Mama and Daddy were talking about something serious, and Patti and I were bored and started to squabble, and Daddy yelled, "If you kids don't cut it out I'm going to knock your heads together!"

Patti and I thought that was funny and we were laughing and Mama was laughing until he came around behind us and with his big hands really did knock our heads together. Then we were both crying and Mama looked like she might cry, too.

My mother wrote in a diary more than a decade later, as the marriage was finally coming apart for good, that my father had never "returned" to her after an extramarital involvement, only left someone else. At any rate, he moved back in with us sometime during my first year of school, and by the end of June Mama was pregnant. We moved again that summer, I started first grade at a new school, and five months after that we were headed to Michigan.

Late in her life, I had a chance to ask my mother why we moved to Michigan when I was six. It had been because my father was "trying to better his situation," she remembered, which meant going to graduate school. (I still don't know why it had to be Michigan and not California.) My mother had looked forward to going back to work and supporting the family, but he changed his mind. "Then he got the chance to get a job at Willow Run—it was a big aircraft factory during the war and then the University of Michigan set up a research facility." He would work and she would take care of the kids (soon to be three), and he would be the man of the house.

We were going to Redlands to see Grandma Dean for Christmas even though it wasn't Christmas yet. Really we were going to say goodbye to her, and after that we were going to keep driving, all the way to Michigan. I had met my grandmother for the first time when I was three and we first arrived in California, and even though visiting her mother always made Mama cranky, I liked Grandma

Dean, and I really liked her house. (My middle name, Hoge, was my grandmother's maiden name, but I was still too little to be self-conscious about it.)

She was standing at the front porch when we drove up, her white braids pinned to the crown of her head, her old blue cardigan over a checked shirtwaist dress, smiling at us. Yes, we could play for a while before supper. She kept a drawer just for Patti and me, with toys and crayons and puzzles, and I found the harmonica and then Patti found the pack of cards and we played War until Grandma said it was time to wash our hands and come to the table. There was going to be a surprise for us after supper.

Grandma Dean always had a clean tablecloth and linen napkins in silver rings and all the silverware and china matched. Patti and I remembered to sit up straight and not grab and to say "please" and "thank you." On one wall hung a painting of a boy with blue eyes and curly blond hair that I knew was my grandfather. He died when my mother was a little girl, and I knew it made Mama sad if I said anything about that. On the other wall there was a tall grandfather clock that didn't have anything do with anybody's grandfather and chimed four times an hour, startling me every time. Patti and I were dressed in matching plaid jumpers and white puffed-sleeve blouses that Grandma Dean had given us. Patti's blond curls contrasted with my limp, light-brown hair, my bangs cut too short and not quite straight. She was already the pretty one.

"Can I have my pusher?" The silver set included pieces just for children, and the pusher looked like a tiny garden hoe with a wide blade, to get food on your fork without using a piece of bread or, for heaven's sake, your fingers. Grandma said I didn't really need it anymore now that I was six and such a big girl, and I was disappointed. That tiny pusher was the part of Grandma Dean's silver set that seemed to belong to me, and it made me feel that I belonged—to something more solid than my immediate family, where sometimes I'd had a sister and sometimes I didn't, once had a father, then didn't, then did again.

"Well, since you're going away, all right." Grandma smiled but looked sad. The grownups were still talking when Patti and I finished and asked to be excused. When Mama came to tell us to put the toys away and get ready to go, Patti put things back in the toy drawer very, very slowly. I told her to hurry up and she said, "Don't you know this is the last time?" I didn't know what she meant and was thinking about the surprise and threw the harmonica back in the drawer and ran to the living room. There was a box by the front door and Grandma Dean opened the top flaps to show us lots and lots of packages, all wrapped in Christmas paper.

"These are for your long trip," she said, and I remembered Mama said it was going to take a week to get to Michigan. The presents had tags and some were for Patti and some were for me and I wondered if there were the same number of packages for each of us, but I didn't ask. "You girls will need to be on your best behavior, so these are something to look forward to. Every day you can each open one of the presents." Daddy wasn't paying attention but Mama was smiling and Patti seemed more cheerful. We gave Grandma a hug and a kiss and climbed into the back seat and Daddy put the box on the floor between us because the way-back was already filled up to the roof.

Back at our house, only the furniture was still there. Patti and I took off our shoes and socks and jumpers but slept in our cotton blouse-slips. It was still dark when Mama woke us up long enough to put our clothes back on and get in the car. We immediately fell back asleep.

When we woke up, we were in the mountains and the sun was coming up.

THE GOOD POETIC MOTHER

"Where are we?"

Mama said we were in the San Bernardino Mountains.

"Is this Mount Baldy? Is it on the way to Camp Radford?" I loved being there with other families from the Unitarian church in Riverside, having fireside sings and marshmallows and sleeping in cabins. I hoped maybe we could go there and not to Michigan, but when Patti asked if we could stop at Camp Radford, Daddy told her not to be ridiculous and Mama said, "Hush, now, Daddy has to concentrate on driving now that we're in the mountains." She always said Daddy was a good driver and there was nothing to be scared of but I had to close my eyes when we went around bends and I thought about the car going over the edge and wondered how long we'd fall.

Now there was snow on the side of the road and Mama said to look how the trees got smaller and more twisted as we drove higher up, and that pretty soon we were going to go over the pass. I didn't know what a pass was or how you got over it, but then the road stopped going up and up and we could see really far in front of us and the clouds were lower than we were. Even Daddy said it was beautiful and stopped so we could get out and look. It was freezing but so pretty that I didn't care. It looked like you could walk on the clouds, but Mama said clouds are just fog and you'd fall through them. I guessed that was a good thing to know but I wished it wasn't true.

After the mountains we'd be in the desert and Patti said if you got stuck out there you'd die of thirst or burn up in the sun or get bitten by rattlesnakes and scorpions. Mama told her to cut it out, but when Daddy stopped to fill the tank Patti read out loud the sign that said, "Last Chance for Gas Before Desert," so I thought maybe she was right. We drove and drove but I still didn't see anything except rocks and dry bushes and small twisty trees. "When do we get to the desert?" I finally asked. They all laughed, and Mama said, "We're in the desert right now!"

Mama said we'd be in Michigan before Christmas, and Patti and I asked her, again, when we were going to come back to Riverside. She said not for a while, but someday for sure, and Daddy said maybe in a couple of years, and Mama said there would be snow in Michigan and wouldn't we like that? When we drove past farms Mama told us to notice the barns and the farmhouses. When we saw a big barn painted bright red, and fields that were neatly plowed, but a farmhouse that didn't look so nice with the paint worn off and one of the shutters hanging crooked, Mama said the farmer was the boss in that family. On another farm there was a big white house with pine trees planted around it and curtains in the windows and a rocking chair on the porch. But the barn needed to be painted and its roof was missing some shingles and Mama said that meant the farmer's wife was the boss in that family. I knew I'd rather live where the farmer's wife was the boss but I didn't say that and I didn't ask who the boss in our family was, either. I knew Mama probably couldn't keep the house nice even if she was in charge, and that anyway whenever Daddy was with us there was only one boss and that was him.

When Patti and I started to bicker Mama told us to lie down and not talk and try to sleep. I watched the telephone wires and after a while it looked like just one wire swooping up and down like a jump rope. As we got farther away from California, the up-and-down wire made me sleepy and Riverside—our house, my first-grade class, Grandma Dean—started to seem like a dream.

LOST AND FOUND (MICHIGAN, 1955)

I had my head down on the table and Mrs. Facing was asking me gently what was wrong and I couldn't stop crying. The other first graders were quiet but I knew the day was ruined, all because of an old black-and-white photograph that I'd wanted to bring for show-and-tell, that I thought I could keep safe. "Make sure you don't lose that," had been the last thing Mama said to me that morning. The snapshot was the size of my hand, with a wavy edge and writing on the back that said *Frances Betty and Helen Mae*. My mother and her little sister, in pretty white dresses, both smiling. It was from before their father died.

I'd been in this class just a few weeks but already had trouble remembering another classroom and another first-grade teacher back in Riverside. When we'd left California my crowded class still didn't have reading books, but in Ypsilanti they'd had *Dick and Jane* for months, and everybody but me could read. I knew my letters and numbers and could print my name and Mrs. Facing had been nice about me not reading. She came to our house after my new sister was

LOST AND FOUND (MICHIGAN, 1955)

born and talked to Mama and saw the baby and said she looked just like Baby Sally in the first grade readers.

I was excited to take my turn at show-and-tell for the first time, and to have something so interesting to show everybody. I thought Mrs. Facing would like me for having it and knowing it was old and precious, and then the other boys and girls would like me because Mrs. Facing did, and maybe things could be all right. I stood up in front of the class in my orange skirt with shoulder straps. Patti had just outgrown the skirt and it was a little big, and my red Mary Janes were a little too small. I told the class that I brought a picture from a long time ago, of my mother and her sister, my Aunt Helen. They were at their grandfather's house in a place called Lexington, Massachusetts. Mama wanted to make sure I explained that part, even though I don't know where Lexington was, but Mrs. Facing nodded and smiled when I said that. I left out the part about their father dying.

Mrs. Facing asked me if I wanted to pass the photograph around, and I didn't know what to say. Finally, she held the picture by the edges and walked around so the other kids could look at it. I sat down and somebody else got up and showed something or told something but I didn't really pay attention. Then it was snack time and we cleared off the tops of our desks and put our papers and pencils inside, and Mrs. Facing brought in the crate with all the cartons of milk—and all of a sudden I didn't have the picture.

It wasn't on my desk and not underneath it, and then things were not all right at all. I wished I'd never brought the picture to class, didn't like this school anymore, wanted to go back to California, thought I hated Mrs. Facing, and definitely hated myself. Mrs. Facing asked if any of the others had seen my picture, but they all shook their heads. She put her hand on my shoulder and gave me a tissue and said we'd find it for sure. If it hadn't turned up by the end of the day I could stay after and she'd help me look for it. I stared hard at the bulletin board where our paintings were tacked up and finally stopped sniffling.

Then Mrs. Facing was saying I could be the one to hand out the milk. I knew she was trying to help me feel better and it sort of helped but mostly didn't. It took a long time to take the cartons from the crate, two at a time, and put them on each desk. Then I had to carry the crate back to the hallway and when I picked it up—

There it was. The photograph was right underneath the milk crate, had been there all the time, was never lost after all. I couldn't believe it and for some reason I wanted to cry again. But Mrs. Facing was smiling and so were the other kids and now I thought they might be my friends and the day started over again.

PICKET LINE (MICHIGAN, 1956)

"The picket line is going to be over there." Mama pointed. We walked around puddles and piles of dirty snow toward a three-story brick apartment building, painted the same color as the old snow. She'd asked me at breakfast if I wanted to go with her to Ann Arbor for a "protest." I wanted to go with her and didn't care much where. I liked Ann Arbor, where we went to church and my father went to classes at night and where there were big trees and beautiful houses. But this didn't look like the part of Ann Arbor I was thinking of.

This morning she'd been talking about a place where Negro families weren't allowed to live. "Do you understand? You know that's not fair, don't you? If you and Patti were little Negro girls, you might not have a place to live." She'd looked at us, hard, and I'd nodded and tried to look serious. I had been worried, because sometimes when she said, "not fair" it meant I had to give up something I wanted.

I didn't know what a picket was and I didn't see a line, but Mama was excited and the other grownups were glad to see her. Somebody handed her a paper cup of coffee and she wrapped her hands around it. I kept my hands in my pockets. The grownups had coffee, and some of them held cigarettes and I could see my breath and pretended I was smoking too. A man with a black beard and red plaid jacket was handing out big cardboard signs on wooden sticks. "Are you big enough to carry one of these?" he asked me. I looked at Mama.

"Oh, yes, she wants her own sign," said Mama, and so I said, "Yes, please." Then I couldn't keep my hands in my pockets, but the man gave me a nice smile and I tried to hold on to the part of the stick that wasn't too splintery. Maybe the stick was a *picket?* Like a picket fence? My sign said, "No More Jim Crow" and I could read that but I didn't know what it meant. It also said "NAACP" and I didn't know that word at all and when Mama said something about "advancement of colored people" I was confused because she'd always made a big deal about how we didn't say "colored," that the right word was "Negro." I wasn't sure about that but I stayed as close to her as I could.

All of a sudden there was a line, and I was in it, and the line was moving and I wasn't sure where Mama was. I tried to look for her but it was hard to do that and keep up with the other grownups and hold my sign straight all at the same time. Then the line made a circle and when I realized we weren't really going anywhere I decided I wouldn't lose Mama after all. The grownups were chanting something over and over and after a few more circles I figured out it was, "No More Jim Crow," like my sign said. I knew we were being fair and good and some other people somewhere else were unfair and bad, and mostly I knew Mama wanted me to do this with her. I wanted to show her I was on her side, and I would pretend that I knew what side that was.

I kept an eye out for Mr. Crow.

FAMILY CAMP (WISCONSIN, 1957)

I was running down the gravely hill to the mess hall, hearing the gong, knowing the way. I remembered it all from the summer before—the canvas platform tents, cool shade under tall oaks, the dock, the lake. What I didn't remember, because they hadn't been there a year before, were the cicadas, their mechanical scream high in the oak branches, crunchy discarded skins littering the path, and glossy green red-eyed monsters inching up tree trunks. The counselors told us about broods and seventeen years underground and miraculous transformations, and I let a giant bug walk on my arm because I wanted the smiling college girl to like me, and she wanted me to be brave.

I was running down the hill and I heard the gong for dinner and I knew the way because we were here last year and the year before that and I was almost nine. I was running and dodging the crisp cicada husks, wearing the brand-new polka dot pedal pushers that Mama sewed for me especially for this week. Mama would be there at mess hall and I knew where to find her and I knew the way.

THE GOOD POETIC MOTHER

I was running down the hill, along the pebbled clay path under the oaks. The ground was littered with acorns, and I forgot to dodge them, and my sneaker slipped, and I was down. My hands stung and my knee throbbed but I scrambled to my feet and at first I was still that brave almost-nine-year-old. Until I looked down and saw blood on my knee and worse, so much worse, a three-cornered tear near the hem of the pedal pushers, and then I was not big and not brave and I wanted Mama. I wasn't sure, not really sure after all, where she was, and I was back in my real life.

From the time I was six until I was almost thirteen, we went to the Unitarian Midwest Summer Assembly at Lake Geneva, Wisconsin for the first week of July. In the bad, and not-so-bad, and really bad years of our parents' marriage, that week was always a miraculous time-out from their usual strife—not just a cease-fire but a period of renewed goodwill and affection. At Lake Geneva my sisters and I were taken care of by people who were trained to do it well, and probably just as important, our mother was cared for herself and not expected to look after anyone else. It reminded her of her own summers at camp and the few happy times she had growing up. My father had no worries about measuring up at work, no dirty house to infuriate him; only relaxation, intellectual stimulation, and admiring friends.

Our parents would begin their transformation as they started packing, becoming the people they were when we went to church or visited their friends. Mama poured black coffee into a thermos, packed sandwiches and snacks we didn't see the rest of the year—chocolate-covered mints, pecan sandy cookies, small cheeses covered

FAMILY CAMP (WISCONSIN, 1957)

in red wax. And a box of foil-wrapped Wash'n Dri wipes for the drive through Chicago—about three-quarters of the way through the day-long drive—because it was always so hot by then. They were relaxed, they were *cheerful*, and we were like other happy families, at least for a week.

My mother was the Unitarian, like her father's Massachusetts family had been for generations. She had gone to youth camp on the Isles of Shoals, where they learned about tides and stars and building a better world, and the experience made an impression that she never forgot. It was because of her that we joined the Unitarian church in Riverside, went on trips with other church families to Camp Radford in the San Bernardino mountains, and, once in Michigan, became members of the Unitarian church in Ann Arbor and discovered Lake Geneva.

The mess hall was huge. Rows of folding chairs were pulled up on both sides of long tables under a high ceiling. Cheerful college girls brought trays to the tables and there was orange juice and milk and hot oatmeal and toast and different kinds of cold cereal, and we could have as much as we wanted. Friends of my parents stopped by our table and the grownups were happy to see each other. Sometimes Daddy put his arm around Mama and they listened to each other and to their friends and laughed together. They even seemed glad to see us when we met them for meals.

That year Pete Seeger was there for the whole week. He ate with us in the mess hall and gave concerts and led singalongs. He was with us, Mama explained, because he was blacklisted and didn't have a job. She reminded us about horrible Joe McCarthy, and talked about the "red scare" and "witch hunts" and if I didn't really understand all that, I knew we liked Pete and we didn't like Ike and we really didn't like something called the "House Un-American Activities Committee."

THE GOOD POETIC MOTHER

Everybody loved Pete. I felt like I knew him already because I could sing the words to most of his songs—not just the baby ones like "Abiyoyo" and "Foolish Frog" but also serious ballads like "One Man's Hands" and "Banks of Marble," and I was always trying to get close to him without being too pushy.

It was almost time for lunch and I was coming up from Junior Swim at the lake and I saw Pete sitting under a tree with his banjo. A lady wearing dungarees and sandals and a plaid madras shirt, with two or three cameras around her neck, waved at me, smiling. "Hi, there! Can you come over here? We need a picture of Pete with some children, would you mind helping out?" My hair was dripping, the blue-and-white striped bathing suit was wet, and I didn't have a t-shirt or even a towel, but this was what I'd been hoping for. Maybe, I'd been imagining, Pete might ask my name and then he'd sing "Goodnight Irene," just for me. The grass was scratchy and it was cold in the shade, but I didn't care. The lady took pictures for a while, moving around the group of kids. The sleeves of Pete's blue work shirt were rolled up past his elbows, and he was strumming and humming. We were all listening, but it wasn't exactly a singalong. Then the lady said she had enough pictures but we should stay for a minute. She told us that she was taking the pictures for *Sing Out!* magazine. Did any of us know what that was? I waved my hand like crazy. "I know, I know!" Mama subscribed to *Sing Out!* and learned new songs from every issue and played her autoharp and sometimes taught us songs like "Dark as a Dungeon" about coal mines, and "All Ye Fair and Tender Ladies," about being careful who you fall in love with, and really I didn't care so much what the songs were about, I was just happy when Mama felt like singing. The camera lady gave each of us a slip of paper, and said we had to get our parents' permission for our pictures to be in the magazine.

FAMILY CAMP (WISCONSIN, 1957)

I spotted Daddy as soon as I got to the mess hall—he was always the tallest in any group—and I ran up to him and showed him the paper and like always I stuttered when I tried to ask him for something, but we were at Lake Geneva and so he had all the patience he never had at home. "Well, that sounds fine," he said, pulling a fountain pen from the pocket of his short-sleeved summer shirt. He signed the permission form, and later on, when the camera lady made an announcement about children in a photograph with Pete, Daddy went over to give her the signed paper and chat with her. They were both smiling and for a minute I was the one who was important.

It was a long time before that photograph of Pete Seeger at Lake Geneva under a tree with children appeared on the cover of *Sing Out!* I was in the picture, sort of, but no one but me would have been able to tell—there was the back of my head, one bare knee, and just the edge of the striped swimsuit I wore that summer. We returned to Lake Geneva three more times, and the final trip was the summer our parents split up. Then those magazines disappeared, along with records, songbooks, the autoharp—and, finally, my mother.

On the Fourth of July there were always fireworks in Williams Bay, just around a point of land from camp. All the families went down to the dock after supper to watch the fireworks blooming overhead and reflected in the dark water. Everybody went "Oooh!," even the grownups. They were being silly like the kids, but the fireworks were really beautiful.

Every summer, I wept when it was time to go home.

SCAPEGOAT (MICHIGAN, 1957)

This time Patti was the one chasing me, and I was the one running too fast. We were eleven and eight, not four and two, but something was about to happen, and it was going to involve a window again. Maybe I had picked up something that belonged to her. I should have known better—Patti hated me and it didn't matter why. For any reason, or even for none, she might trip me, or back me into a corner and kick my shins so that they were black and blue a lot of the time, but Mama wouldn't get involved.

Patti was behind me and I was running from our bedroom down the hall to the living room and I turned to the right because the other direction led to Mama and the kitchen and it would be safer, I thought, to try to get out the front door. I swerved but Patti didn't turn in time and ran smack into the picture window. There was a terrible crash and a big piece of glass was outside on the dirt and another piece hung from the top of the window like the blade of a guillotine and everything stopped for a moment.

Mama ran in and screamed at Patti. "Get away from that window right now!" We had to stand in the corner and stay there until our father got home.

Patti told me over and over that I was the worst person in the world, and that if I didn't know it I was just stupid, because everybody else did. "Everybody talks about you all the time," she told me, as if this were serious news and she had a duty to make sure I knew it. "You're fat and ugly and your hair is dishwater." Patti's hair was a true blond, and her eyes were bluer than mine, and I had always known that she was the prettier one. That wasn't news.

"And you're adopted, you know." She never let up on this one, either, never said, "Just kidding." I thought it might not be so bad to be adopted, because it would mean that I didn't really belong there and might find my real family someday.

My mother herself was the older of two sisters, and it seemed to me that she always took Patti's side. She insisted she loved us both exactly the same, and maybe she believed she did, but in a journal I discovered after her death I read her account of how she felt about little sisters in general, and about her sister Helen in particular.

June 23, 1961.

There is a four-year-old boy down the street here who keeps trying to kill Donna, who is the same age (two years) as his younger sister. This little sister has what he wants—his mother's love, his father's approval... I can barely remember pushing Helen over that bluff. Or telling her I thought her "the most disgusting person in the world." Or trying to push her out my bedroom win-

dow. But I can remember pretty well trying to kill her with my fist, in the kitchen, and hurting my shoulder. And going at her with the ski pole, in the woods.

Frances Dean Smith (Journal)

School was just as bad as home. Nobody played with me at recess. I walked around the edge of the playground, didn't go on the monkey bars since the time a boy tried to push me off and everybody else laughed. It seemed like the other kids in third grade thought there was something bad about me, too, and I didn't know if they'd started it or if Mrs. Andrews had. Back in the classroom we had a worksheet to fill out, and I couldn't find my pencil. I had to raise my hand, and Mrs. Andrews was not nice about it. "Class, does anyone have a pencil for this poor, pitiful girl who can't remember to bring her pencils to school?" I wanted to cry but I knew that would make things worse.

I had to walk home from school as fast as I could because there were kids who hid behind the big tree at the edge of the schoolyard and if I ran they'd chase me. Nobody hit me but they pretended they were going to and screamed with laughter when I flinched. I ran the last half-block and mostly tried not to think about school if I could help it.

The only good place, really, was church. Mama was never up in time to get us to Sunday school but her friend Mrs. Cohen came by to pick Patti and me up and take us to Ann Arbor. Patti smiled and used her nice voice, and answered questions about the baby and why Mama wasn't up yet but would come later and yes, we'd meet our parents at coffee hour and no, Mrs. Cohen wouldn't have to give us a ride home. Once we were at church Patti and I were in different classes, and in mine I had a friend.

Sally Adams had been in the same Sunday school class with me since first grade, and I always hoped she'd ask me to come over to her house for what her mother called dinner but was really lunch. It was like Thanksgiving every Sunday—Mrs. Adams made a chicken or roast beef and always mashed potatoes and even rolls, and the whole family sat together and Mr. Adams made jokes and said how good the food was. I wanted to live with them forever.

In my real life in Ypsilanti, Patti and I helped with two-year-old Sara, usually made supper, and always had to do the dishes. Patti washed and I dried and once Daddy took a glass out of the cupboard and held it up to the light to show us it was streaky. "No wonder everybody keeps getting sick around here! These dishes are filthy!" It was true that Patti had the flu and then I got it and when I got better Sara was sick and Mama just didn't get out of bed for a while, but I didn't know it was because I hadn't dried the dishes right. Anyway, Patti was the one washing. But I didn't say that, because he would have yelled at us some more and then Patti would beat me up the first chance she got and Mama would probably cry.

We moved to South Grove Road the summer I turned eight. It was the first house our parents owned, and for a while they both seemed happy there. Years later, I learned that they had been able to buy that house because my mother came into a trust fund her grandfather Dean had left her, and that it had been my father who really wanted to own a home. My mother wrote, in the journal she kept at the end of the marriage, that he had been, "trying to fit some dream he had of being just like other men only not working so hard at it," and I remember him as perpetually angry. Then a fourth baby was on the way, and his father died back in California, and he got even meaner for a while.

ANXIOUS ATTACHMENT (MICHIGAN, 1960)

I didn't know where Mama was. Maybe I was supposed to know what she was doing that afternoon, but I just knew I was hungry and that it had been a long windy walk from the bus stop and that I'd been thinking all the way up the hill about how pleased she would be that I took the bus by myself. I let myself in, dropped my book bag on the table, and tried to figure out if anybody was home.

Mama didn't get why I hated to take the bus and I couldn't explain it. I'd started worrying even before I left the house this morning: *Is the fare still twenty-five cents? Do I have quarters in my pocket? Are they still there? It's the 12B, I know that. I thought I knew that. Unless it's 12A. No, I'm sure it's the 12B. Except how will I know if I've already missed it, and when will the next one come? If I get on the wrong bus I could end up in Ypsilanti or even Detroit.*

The boxy black-and-white 12B stopped on Miller Road about five minutes after I got down the hill, and as it rumbled toward town my heart gradually stopped pounding in my ears. When I saw the first red-roofed university buildings I started watching for the arch at the corner of the quad, but everything looked different from inside the bus. I was supposed to get off at the corner of South University and East University, I knew that, but at State Street I saw the Carillon and got confused again. *What if we've already passed my stop?* I should have gone up front and asked the driver, but then everybody would have looked at me. *There's the arch. There's Ulrich's bookstore.* I pulled the cord and the bus slowed to a stop and then I was on the sidewalk. For a minute I was sure I'd made a mistake, but I was looking the wrong way—when I turned around I saw the school steps halfway down the next block. I didn't catch my breath until I got to homeroom.

Now it was almost four o'clock, getting dark out and even darker inside, and no one was at home. Across the living room the four windows glowed deep blue in the twilight, reminding me of something that I wanted to ask Mama about. *The blue time? A perfume? A poem she wrote?* When I switched on the light, indigo turned to black and all I saw was the reflected scene: me in my blue pullover, pleated gray skirt, bobby socks, and white sneakers, the living room, the kitchen, orange countertops, newspapers and books on the table. *Where is she?* I hoped there was something to eat. *Maybe she's at class? Which class?* I was pretty sure there was some instant cocoa. *I'd like to go with her to pottery class again.* I ran water into the scuffed aluminum kettle, put it on the electric stove, found a heavy white china mug in the sink, rinsed it out. I was glad Mama was happy, but it seemed like she was always out now. Modern dance, Russian language, planning to take creative writing. She'd been wearing lipstick and putting something on her hair called a rinse.

In the back of a lower cupboard I found the red box of Nestle's EverReady, at least half full, and started to breathe again.

❖ ❖ ❖

ANXIOUS ATTACHMENT (MICHIGAN, 1960)

By the end of the 1950s our father had finished his master's degree and left Willow Run Labs for a promotion and a job on campus. He was more cheerful and less scary after he started going to work in Ann Arbor, and that seemed to change everything at home. They weren't fighting so much, Mama had friends and was happier, Patti and I didn't have to take care of our sisters all the time, and Patti stopped being so mean to me. I started to forget about the worst times in the Ypsilanti house. And there must have been more money and enough hope that they decided they could build a beautiful new house in a nice part of Ann Arbor.

We were moving up, I thought. Leaving Ypsilanti for Ann Arbor, moving from a cramped bungalow near the Ford plant to a bigger modern house in a pretty neighborhood, exchanging a bare dirt yard for a real lawn, and I was getting out of public school and into the University School. We might finally be one of those "good" families.

Mama had been excited all during the construction. When a gigantic boulder came out of the excavation she got the bulldozer man to move it to the back yard, planned to grow bachelor buttons, Queen Anne's lace and purple vetch all around what she had started calling, "my rock." She picked out pumpkin-orange countertops and found a dramatic black stain for the vertical support beam in the middle of the house. Our new four-bedroom was as nice as the other ones in the neighborhood, or it was going to be when Daddy got the foundation painted and when Mama planted the Japanese maple tree out front. She even made curtains (instead of just buying fabric and saying she'd get around to it) by sewing pleat tape across the top of new white sheets, putting in the four-pronged hooks that made gathers like machine-made drapes. Daddy put up real curtain rods and I helped Mama draw free-form flowers on the bottom edge of the sheets with magic markers, and they looked surprisingly nice.

She was cheerful, making things, full of plans. I forgot to worry about her for a while.

I had always remembered the house we'd lived in when I was born as almost a castle, with its striking round tower, but it was a typical corner row house in the Capitol Hill neighborhood of Washington, D.C.—the area was working-class back then, and my grandmother rented out rooms. After we left Michigan, I developed a similarly aggrandized image of our last home there, imagining the low-slung yellow rambler near the crest of Morningside Drive as larger and more dramatically beautiful than it really was. It had the shallow-angled roof that says *contemporary*, cathedral ceilings, and clerestory windows—elongated scalene triangles just below the roofline—and was spacious and attractive, especially compared to anywhere we'd lived before, but not really grand. Ann Arbor has a rich architectural heritage of mid-century modern houses. Those iconic lines, expanses of glass, and pleasing simplicity became conflated, after we left, with memories of the actual house we lived in for just two and a half years.

They had a housewarming party. Mama put on her silver earrings and a narrow-waisted black dress, and served angel food cake with frozen strawberries and sour cream. I thought sour cream sounded like a good way to ruin strawberries and cake, but it was delicious. Like the curtains, the orange counters, the black post in the living room—I hadn't been sure she knew what she was doing, but it turned out to be exactly what she had in mind, and just right.

ANXIOUS ATTACHMENT (MICHIGAN, 1960)

They hadn't had a really bad fight since we left Ypsilanti. She still didn't always get up on time, but she didn't stay in bed all day, either. Patti had the alarm clock, and I got out of bed when I heard it from the next room and put cornflakes, milk and sugar, four cereal bowls and four spoons on the table while Patti woke the little kids up. Sara was in kindergarten, and could dress herself and help Ruthie, too, and usually they were ready by the time the car pool came. I was in seventh grade, had some friends, and was starting to feel pretty good about my new school. I drew a peace sign in ballpoint pen on my olive-green canvas book bag and slung it over my shoulder just the way Patti and her ninth-grade friends did. I tried to forget Ypsilanti, and hoped that this tenth move would be the last.

At Christmas our parents were happy, although I had been on edge all day, waiting for the first impatient words, a quarrel escalating to yelling, crying, and four girls running to separate corners of the house—the Christmas tradition we'd grown up with. Mama sat smiling, legs crossed in the orange canvas butterfly chair. In a tweed jacket with leather patches on the elbows, Daddy leaned back on black leather, put his feet up on the matching ottoman, and lit his pipe. They talked and joked after the presents. Kennedy was going to the White House; their friend Mr. Cohen had landed a position in the new administration. She'd gotten over Stevenson and didn't sneer about Kennedy any more. He said something about a leave of absence from the university, about a job "on the hill." She said it was too soon to tell the kids. I didn't know what a leave of absence was or what hill they were talking about and somehow I didn't want to ask.

THE GOOD POETIC MOTHER

In January, they told us that there would be another move. We agreed to believe them when they said it was only for a while, that after a year or two in D.C. we would certainly, definitely, absolutely move back to Ann Arbor. Daddy was going to Washington right after the inauguration, but we wouldn't have to leave until the end of the school year.

I stopped expecting to find Mama at home in the afternoons. She was taking a class in creative writing and another in Russian and I came home one day toward the end of winter to find the living room windows lined with Cyrillic letters painted in robin's-egg blue. "Yevtushenko," she said. "The most beautiful poetry in the world. Much better to read it in the original Russian."

Maybe in Ann Arbor it was okay to have Russian words on the windows, I hoped. I knew about the poetry and the Russian and even the literary magazine she was helping to revive. I couldn't know, of course, how little time was left.

Mama was smoking, pacing, clutching a cup of black coffee, and I wanted to talk to her. It had been exciting at first to think of Washington and the Kennedys, and I'd thought it would be fun and might make me more interesting if I went away for a year and came back. But now that the school year was ending, I was starting to feel sad. I really didn't want to miss being in eighth grade with my friends. I was tired of being cooperative and was ready for an argument.

"I still don't get why we have to move."

She sighed, but I had more to say.

"I've only been at U High for one grade! That's not fair—Patti's had three whole years. I finally have friends and Mr. Berg said I

ANXIOUS ATTACHMENT (MICHIGAN, 1960)

should try out for choir next year, but I won't even be here!" I started to get even more upset than I'd thought I was. She seemed willing to hear me out. Maybe I could convince her we should all stay here and Daddy could keep coming home every other weekend and not make us move.

Mama stopped pacing and looked at me, tilting her head to the side, almost smiling. "I know you like school now, but that's just because you have a better attitude. University School's not so special. You just don't want things to change. Lots of people are afraid of change." This sounded like one of her speeches about how narrow-minded most people are, but so far she still seemed sort of sympathetic. "There'll be a choir at your new school, or at church. You'll find new things to like. You'll make lots of new friends."

That wasn't helping. "I don't want new friends; I want to live here! This is the best place we've ever lived. I don't see why we have to leave!"

"It's not forever," she went on. "We'll come back, I told you that. That's why we're just renting the house and not selling it."

I'd heard that before. "When exactly are we coming back, then? By ninth grade? Can you promise it'll be exactly one year?"

"I said we'll come back. Your father's on leave. He has to come back." She wasn't so patient, getting a bit sharp.

"Well, how long *exactly*?"

"I don't know *exactly*! You're making too big a deal out of it, going on like that. Don't be stupid."

It was probably her saying I was stupid that did it. Daddy said that all the time but usually she said, "Of course not, you know you're really smart but he's in a bad mood and stay out of his way." But I was so mad that I said what I'd been thinking since they first told us about moving. "Well, isn't that what you said when we left Riverside? And that didn't happen, did it? When we came to Michigan you promised we'd be moving back to California, and did we? No, and we never will, either! So why should we believe—"

    I didn't realize what the look on her face meant and was in the middle of a sentence when she put her coffee cup down, switched the cigarette to her left hand, and slapped me across the face, hard. My plastic harlequin-framed glasses flew across the kitchen, I started to cry and she started to yell. "Don't say that!" and "How dare you?" and "You little shit!" and "I've had it with you!" I didn't hear the rest because I was running away and down the stairs to the basement and my bedroom. I slammed the door and put my fingers in my ears so I couldn't hear if she was still yelling.

FATHER'S DAY (MICHIGAN, 1961)

"If your mother is serious about this," my father said, "what do you want to do? Stay with her, or go with me?"

Her. Or him. He was right there, and she was somewhere else. He was the exciting, elusive parent, while my mother, as I moved from childhood toward adolescence, had become increasingly annoying. Going with him meant Washington, and saying, "My father works on Capitol Hill." Staying with her meant having to tell my friends, "We're not going to Washington after all, and no you can't come over, because my mother's not up yet and the house is a disaster and she's so—" I didn't know what to say she was.

Our father had been in Washington since January and had a very important job about which I knew nothing except that it clearly impressed my parents' friends. I hoped it would impress my own friends if I could only explain what exactly he was doing. We'd been packing since school let out, getting ready for the move. It was only going to be for a year or two, and I had convinced myself that we would be coming back.

THE GOOD POETIC MOTHER

When my father arrived for the weekend things were still a mess. The living room lined with cartons, some empty, some partly filled, heaps of unsorted laundry scattered across the hallway floor, newspapers piled on the table, and dirty dishes stacked up to the faucet in the once-bright stainless steel sink. My own basement bedroom wasn't much better—I'd packed some clothes and most of my books and then had to unpack the box to find my teddy bear, which I was too old for but couldn't sleep without.

Family camp was always the first week of July. This year, I was going to be in the junior high dorm with kids my age, and when I got too nervous about going to Washington I thought about Lake Geneva and felt better.

But the family that was going to rent our house would be arriving in July, which meant we had to be moved out before we went to Lake Geneva and the packing had a real deadline. Mama wasn't happy about any of this and for days had been impatient with all of us. "We have to be packed in a week. Your father's going to be here in five days." I tried to avoid her as much as I could.

Daddy got in on Saturday, and within an hour they were fighting. Their usual *what's wrong with you, you're crazy, no you're crazy* routine, followed by shouts back and forth, slammed doors, curses. But this time after his familiar, "I can't take this anymore," she had a different retort.

"Well, don't, then."

By the time my sisters and I went to bed, our parents were having a serious talk beyond the closed bedroom door.

On Sunday morning he was cheerful, as if nothing had happened. But inevitably something didn't go right, she got on his nerves, and we registered his irritation even before he started in on her. "So when

FATHER'S DAY (MICHIGAN, 1961)

exactly were you planning to finish packing these boxes?" She didn't answer.

"I'm wondering when you're going to get this mess sorted out." Still no reply.

"Are you planning to leave it all until next week? You're even crazier than I thought you were!"

And then we heard her say, "Well, actually, I don't think I'll do it next week. Next week I plan to be seeing a lawyer. About the divorce." We ran away, but the shouting did not resume.

For a while there was silence, then conversation too faint to hear, then a prolonged quiet and an uncanny feeling in the pause between cataclysm and the resumption of ordinary life. Sara and Ruthie murmured together in their room, Patti sulked in hers. I waited in my bedroom for something to happen.

Then my father came to find me, to talk to me alone. A tall man, he wore his dark-blond hair in a crew cut, as he had since the Army. He had the long fingers, high-arched feet and blue eyes that my sisters and I all shared, and people thought him good looking, smart, and generally quite impressive. He seldom had anything to say directly to any of us, his pronouncements were usually directed at *you kids*—as in, "You kids better shape up!"— and I couldn't remember the last time I had an actual conversation with him. He was the parent who never took notice, never approved, who was both frightening and desirable, and in his presence I instinctively tried to be whatever I imagined he wanted me to be. I was afraid of him, as always, but hoped his attention meant he liked me after all. I was very good at figuring out what he wanted, and I heard a small voice reply, "With you, I guess."

I could tell by his expression that I had given the right answer, and was relieved. Then he told me (it would have been simpler had he said this first), that Patti had also chosen to go with him. I decided I had made the right choice. I decided it was my own choice. I began to recalculate my future.

ROUND ONE (WASHINGTON, 1961)

The first iteration of child custody took place in the summer and fall of 1961, a period where my memories are even more confused and fragmented than the disorganized recollections of the rest of my early life. I mis-remembered important parts of that situation until after my mother died and I discovered her journal. The incomplete and partly-false memory I had seems to have been strongly influenced by what my parents had told us was going to happen—that Patti and I would live with our father in Washington, our little sisters in Michigan with our mother. But, even though I can't really remember them there (and this makes me uneasy), Sara and Ruthie were in D.C. all that fall, with our father and Patti and me, on Third Street, Southwest, in a brand-new townhouse. He told us the neighborhood was called *New Southwest*, part of something called *urban renewal*, and he was pleased with himself to have found a place there. When Mama first saw the modern three-level tan brick townhouse in its row of other pastel units, she'd been skeptical, wondering where all the people who used to live here went when their neighborhood got

THE GOOD POETIC MOTHER

"renewed." But then she wasn't there and I didn't know when she might be with us again.

It turns out that even before the dramatic Father's Day fight, when she first proposed a separation, she had been ambivalent about leaving Ann Arbor behind completely and was trying to find a compromise between her writing life and the obligations of marriage and motherhood.

June 11, 1961.

The church picnic... a beautiful warm summer day (the kind that always peaks, as this one did, to a terrible storm at five) and I in my plaid shorts and grey shirt, dirty and comfortable and full of tears, found a way to mourn and make my peace.... Everyone hopes I'll have a good time in Washington. "You'll find it very stimulating, as a writer." I try to explain just how over-stimulating I find it, how impossible it is to take in more than a very little bit at a time of that drifting, lonesome scene, how luxury affects me....

If I live in Washington from Friday to Monday as well as I can, I can expect to get... some thinking and writing done from Tuesday through Thursday as I travel to Ann Arbor and back for class. Wouldn't it be heaven if I found the bus schedules possible for half the trips, the night air coach financially possible one trip in three?

Frances Dean Smith, (Journal)

ROUND ONE (WASHINGTON, 1961)

I knew I was dreaming even as I hurried down one wrong hallway after another, searching for the eighth-grade classroom, trying to wake up, turning another corner and *there's the bell and I'm already late*—and then I did wake up and the alarm clock said 7:30. I reached down to pick it up from the floor and stop the noise. I wasn't in the dream anymore, but for a few moments I didn't know where I was.

I lay still for a few minutes trying to remember who was where. Patti's bed on the other side of our shared half-basement room was empty and I remembered she had to catch an early bus to get to Western High School, in some other part of the city. Daddy was, of course, already at work. And Mama was somewhere else. Sometime in August she had been in D.C. long enough to go down to the Vital Records office for copies of birth certificates for me and Patti (we'd both been born in Washington). Before she left again for wherever she went, she had taken me to register at Thomas Jefferson Junior High, where we stood at the foot of a flight of limestone steps rising to three sets of double doors and an imposing red brick building with tall white-mullioned windows and a copper-roofed white cupola. Above four two-story columns, bronze letters said JEFFERSON JUNIOR HIGH. I'd asked Mama if she thought it would be anything like U High, and she raised one skeptical eyebrow. "Well, it's just through grade nine. But it will be good for you to go to a city school. You'll be exposed to different kinds of people. And it's integrated, that's the great thing."

Mama had not been impressed with the fact that Jefferson had a "dress code," although Daddy seemed to think it somehow signified a superior education. Girls had to wear either dresses or skirts and blouses; no culottes, curlers, sneakers or sandals. Skirts had to be an "appropriate" length. None of that sounded very different from how we dressed back home, without any rules, so it wasn't one of the things I worried about.

I found a black cotton turtleneck, hoped it was still clean and realized it would have to do, since I really didn't have anything else. I was glad to have the tan poplin jumper I'd made in seventh grade home economics class. I knew how to sew even before getting to home ec, and had done a good job on the jumper. The darts were matched up, all the seams were bound, and the hem was straight. I wore my not-quite-too-small Capezio flats and black tights and the tiny ebony-and-silver earrings I'd bought with my own money at Bob Marshall's bookstore back in Ann Arbor. It was an outfit I'd worn before, the kind of thing Patti and her friends and now some of mine, too, wore—more grown up than the bobby socks and full skirts of seventh grade. I thought I looked nice and felt a bit less nervous.

I made sure the front door locked behind me, then hurried down Third Street, right on I Street, and then right on Seventh to the fenced area at the back of the school. Mama and I hadn't gotten any further than the school office when I registered, but the lady there had made sure I understood that students were *not* allowed to use the grand front entrance, so I crossed the blacktop on the not-so-nice side of the school and climbed the iron stairs. There was a teacher standing outside the office and I showed her my registration form. She looked me up and down, frowning, then at the piece of paper, and finally pointed down the hall, where I found the classroom that had the same number as my list. The other kids were still coming in and sitting down, and I went up to the front trying not to think about everybody looking at me, and showed the teacher my form. She seemed startled and stared at me with obvious confusion. "Take that seat by the window, then."

It was in the first row. I wished I could sit at the back.

I looked around as much as I could without actually turning my head. I didn't see any White kids at all and I didn't know how to feel about that.

The teacher introduced herself to the class. I remember her kind eyes, light-brown complexion, and soft curls, but haven't the ghost of a memory of her name. She welcomed back those who had been at Jefferson for seventh grade, and "new students, too," with a friendly glance in my direction. She was going over the school rules, had a lot to say about "appropriate behavior," about coming to school "ready to learn," showing respect to teachers and staff.... I gradually tuned out.

I would get off on the right foot here, I vowed. I'd done pretty well in seventh grade and I would make sure to keep up with my homework this year. Even if I was different from everybody else, maybe I could still be a good kid, the smart one who is nice to the other students and doesn't act stuck up. Then the teachers might be happy to have me in their classes and would think I set a good example, and if I did really well in school, my father would notice. Maybe it could work out that way.

My thoughts drifted to where I'd been last spring, seeing Ann Arbor in a golden light of nostalgia—the collegiate-gothic school building on the University of Michigan campus, with broad front steps and a two-story library with tall stained-glass windows, big trees in the lawn out back, the grassy interior courtyard. Caught in my reverie, I wasn't alarmed when someone came to the classroom door, spoke to the teacher, and beckoned me out into the hall. Two women were there and I assumed they had a question about my registration. I was used to having to fill in information that that my mother hadn't included on some form, and I smiled to show them I was glad to be helpful.

Neither of them smiled back. The taller woman, frowning behind black cats-eye eyeglasses, had her arms folded and was practically tapping her foot. The shorter one, gray curls rigid with hairspray, stared at me without expression, and I began to perspire in the cool, dark hallway. They took turns: "…a shame we have to speak to you about your attitude on your first day here …expect students to be ladies and gentlemen… be aware of the rules… behave correctly… dress in an appropriate way."

Was there something wrong with what I was wearing? I looked down—my jumper was clean and only a little wrinkled, and I thought my shoes looked nice with the black tights. I didn't think there was a rule against wearing jewelry. I looked at one of the women, then the other. Both of them seemed angry, or disgusted, or both.

"… a serious infraction… you could be sent home… you're new here and so we'll give you a second chance…. And don't make us have to speak to you again, do you understand?"

"I understand," I said. But I didn't understand anything. I went back into the classroom and sat down. A couple of kids were snickering and the teacher told them to be quiet. I couldn't figure out what had just happened. The room was swimming, but I didn't let myself cry. I can't remember now what I wore to school the next day.

For years I tried not to think about that day, and whenever I did remember it, I felt again the old shame and hopelessness and lingering confusion about what it was exactly that I was supposed to have done wrong. I've wondered many times what those women thought I was trying to do—since they clearly thought I *was* trying to get away with something. Maybe they thought I was trying to look like a "beatnik," but that doesn't really hold up when I recall my thirteen-year-old self and the homemade jumper. Did they think I was trying to seem better than the others?

I'll never know, and have to form my own account. I've come to believe that there were probably two factors at play. One is that the real, although unspoken, purpose of the dress code was to enforce conformity. Even if my clothes fit the letter of the dress code, I looked like what I was—a girl from a university town up north, who identified with, and dressed like, her older sister and her mother, who wanted to carry some bit of her old self to this strange place. They might have seen me as willfully refusing to fit in.

The other factor, harder to acknowledge or accept, also had to do with looking different. I think that the women who confronted me that day may have been ready to dislike me; in a school that was still nearly all-Black, despite desegregation, a new White girl might be resented, and not only by other students. They had to let me in, but they didn't have to be nice to me.

That's the part of the problem that I had no way of understanding. I held the attitudes and beliefs about race that my parents seemed to have—a vague, northern liberal, benevolent, and unconsciously condescending stance. I knew that some people were unfair to "Negroes" (as I'd been taught to say), even believed they weren't as good as White people. Intelligent people knew better than that, and should try to help Negroes because they were *disadvantaged*. If Negroes could get the same opportunities as everybody else, life would be fairer and the Negro people would be grateful. That muddle of unexamined assumptions may have supported a highly unrealistic expectation that I would actually be welcomed at this just-integrated school.

I don't really know what my parents thought. My father was working for a Black congressman, had decided to live in the new neighborhood that was someday going to be integrated, even if it still wasn't. Maybe I was his way of walking the walk. My mother, I think, believed it was possible to be completely color blind. She tried to be that way herself, and that might have been all right, if she hadn't been blind about so many other things.

May 18, 1961.

Later when we sat and talked, he told me that he believes we should stay together, he wants his family with him, he's not going back without us.... He wants the children in the very best schools but can't say what he hopes their education will mean in their lives, he wants them with him but hasn't thought about whether or not they'll have company, art and music, help in understanding the city, any of that he just hasn't thought about at all. He's a good father, ask anybody, why am I quizzing him, he doesn't call them names half as much as he used to. When I talk, telling him my most personal thoughts and dreams about the kids... he is not hearing, though I'm talking truly and directly to him.

Anyway, maybe he will remember later.

Frances Dean Smith (Journal)

I have always remembered writing a letter to my mother during what had to have been the third week of September, 1961. A two-inch headline in the *Washington Post* one Tuesday morning upset me more than seemed to make sense, and I was still thinking about it when I got back to the townhouse after school. *Dag Hammarskjöld Dies in African Air Crash / Lone Survivor Reports Explosions.*

We got two newspapers—the *Washington Post* was delivered in the morning and our father brought the *Washington Star* home after work.

ROUND ONE (WASHINGTON, 1961)

Mama had said the *Post* was much better than the *Star*, and I read more of that paper than I ever had of the *Ann Arbor News*, feeling sophisticated and grown up. But the real reason I read it is that there were no books in my father's house and I didn't have a library card and I didn't know where the library was and probably wasn't allowed to go there anyway.

Dag Hammarskjöld was a name I recognized. We'd learned about the United Nations in seventh grade, and I knew Mama thought the United Nations was a good thing because if she ever managed to send Christmas cards it was always the UNICEF kind, and she liked it if we took the orange penny-collection boxes along for trick or treat. I knew the UN was good because it was for peace, and Mr. Hammarskjöld was good because he was from Sweden where they didn't believe in war, and Mama and I liked Scandinavian furniture and anything from the Midnight Sun store in Ann Arbor. And also, Mama said, Dag Hammarskjöld was a poet. Like she used to be. Like maybe she was again.

I read that President Kennedy said Hammarskjöld was a "great statesman" and then I was suddenly sad, close to tears, as if somebody I knew had died, and that didn't make any sense. All I knew was that my chest hurt and I couldn't swallow right. I didn't say anything to Patti—she ignored almost anything I said—and I didn't talk to Daddy because he was gone in the morning before I got up and usually home around the time I went to bed and brought work home and didn't want to be bothered, before work or after work.

So I decided to write to Mama. Some of the things we'd brought from Ann Arbor were still in boxes in the furnace room, and after I dug through two of them I found the stationary that I remembered. The pale blue paper was almost too nice to use, so there was still a lot of it left. I borrowed Patti's ballpoint pen, the one that didn't skip and wrote a really thin line and made my handwriting look more grown up.

Dear Mama,

I just read the terrible news about Mr. Hammarskjöld. President Kennedy said he was a great statesman and I know you admire him a lot. I'm thinking of you and hope you are all right. I am very sad about it. I hope there will still be a United Nations after this.

I am fine. School is fine. We are going to have dinner at Nanny's this weekend, on Friday, or if Daddy has to work then on Saturday.

Love,

Irene

(I must have sent this letter to the Morningside Drive house. It had only been rented out for the summer, the renters would have been gone by fall, and I now assume that's where my mother stayed when she wasn't with us.)

When I came home from school on Friday I found a letter for me from Mama. I didn't want Patti to see it, so I took it to our bedroom and put it under my pillow. I went back upstairs to make sure Patti wasn't home yet, and then remembered she'd be late—something about decorating for a dance at school. So I poured some milk and made toast and got the letter and sat down at the table.

The address was typed, to "Irene Hoge Smith." Mama was the only person who ever used my middle name and I kind of wished she wouldn't. The letter was typed, too. Only her signature was written by hand, with a kind of flourish underneath it.

I no longer have that letter, but remember it went something like this:

ROUND ONE (WASHINGTON, 1961)

Dearest Irene,

It is always so nice to get a letter from you. Maybe you would also like to send me other things you write sometime. You should try writing poetry. I'm sure you would love that.

About Hammarskjöld, I guess I did have high hopes for him at one time but in recent years he unfortunately seemed to have become just another politician. I'm not surprised Kennedy says he was "great" because really they are both the same kind of stuffed shirt. I think I'm really done with politics. Even Stevenson seems pretty washed up now. Of course I'm not glad that Hammarskjöld died, but to be honest it didn't mean much to me.

I've been meaning to send you a book of Yevtushenko's poetry. Do you think your school library has his books? If you can't find them let me know and maybe I can send you a copy of something. You should look at a Russian version sometime, even though you can't read it. Just the alphabet is so very beautiful it makes me cry.

    lots of love
        from your
            Mama

My chronology of 1961 is spotty. As best as I can piece it together, there was a back-and-forth about divorce that began in mid-June, when my mother said they should separate. My father didn't believe she was serious, argued, said he wanted his family with him, and thought he'd changed her mind. When he realized she hadn't, he took all four girls with him to D.C. and left my mother behind in Ann Arbor.

THE GOOD POETIC MOTHER

At the end of the month he drove us back to Michigan, and we all, including our mother, went to Wisconsin for a week at family camp. He had to leave early, but pleaded again with my mother.

July 5, 1961.

About 3:00 A.M. Back from the airport. He asked questions and made all kinds of last-minute pleas for reconsideration. Tears. Seems he never quite believed before that I was serious. I shook his hand and told him he was great, and I believe it is barely possible that he will not put up too much of a fight. I don't trust him, but that is my best informed guess about it just the same.

Frances Dean Smith (Journal)

After Lake Geneva I was in D.C. with my sisters and our father for the rest of the summer, and our mother wasn't. She told me years later, "He moved to D.C. and I went to California to visit my mom and sister. And then I went to stay with him in D.C. with you kids." I'll never know what she thought was going to happen next, or if she was surprised when my father changed his mind again at the end of August.

August 26, 1961.

He says he really thinks that he and I should get a divorce; to explain me to the outside world or to himself, as his wife, is just too difficult for him, it's something he cannot do. He says the reason is, he knows, in him, his own worries and frustrations and his terrors. Where will I go? I think perhaps I should go to Riverside.... I will take Ruthie, I'll have to. And I should, but I don't see how I can, take Sara.

ROUND ONE (WASHINGTON, 1961)

August 29 (?) in Findlay, Ohio - not even halfway - oh yes we are, we must be: I am so in despair it's unbearable.
Frances Dean Smith (Journal)

Perhaps it was sometime in the three days between my father's pronouncement and her next departure (this time, I think, to go with Unitarian church friends to a camp in northern Michigan) that she tried to kill herself again. She never wrote of this, but did describe to me a scene of which I recall only an image and a feeling—the kitchen in the D.C. townhouse, someone on the floor, panic, and a stick of butter. She drank a bottle of gin, and I was the one who found her, of that part she was sure. She made me give her the butter, maybe in the belief that eating it would ward off alcohol poisoning. Perhaps it did, because she survived. I was thirteen when that happened, the age she'd been when she tried to hang herself from her grandfather's apple tree.

ROUND TWO (MICHIGAN, 1962)

This must be the rest stop, I thought. It was hard to understand the driver's announcements over the staticky public address system, but outside the rain-streaked window a yellow sign read *Midway Service Plaza*, and as I shepherded Sara and Ruthie toward the exit I could hear the driver more clearly. "We'll pull out in twenty minutes. Anybody not on the bus by then will be spending the night at Midway."

My sisters had been sleeping most of the time since we got on the bus. Maybe that had been the rationale for letting the three of us travel without an adult—they'd be asleep and I could handle them easily and it was just one bus and no transfers and wasn't I old enough to be in charge? I was thirteen and a half, in junior high, and had on (for some reason I can no longer reconstruct) one of my mother's dresses, the kind of stylish, pretty frock she'd mostly stopped wearing. Had it been the only thing I *could* wear? Had I outgrown what few outfits I had? Or had I chosen to dress up in this dark-red plaid linen dress, with its fitted bodice and slender matching belt and full skirt and—

ROUND TWO (MICHIGAN, 1962)

In the ladies' room mirror I saw that something wasn't right about the dress. I looked down, and realized with dismay that a long length of hem had come undone, that the skirt was uneven and drooping, and my fragile imitation of adulthood had collapsed, revealing what I really was—a scared, scruffy kid, trying to take care of two even younger children.

I have always had the memory of being on a bus with my little sisters, somewhere between Washington and Michigan. The scene always included the rain and worrying about getting my sisters back on the bus before it left without us, and the heartbreak of the pretty dress and the ugly torn hem. But I have never been able to work out whether we were going to D.C. or to Ann Arbor and why it was just the three of us. This memory lapse is just one ill-fitting piece in the impossible puzzle of the months before and after the end of my parents' marriage. I was there, but perhaps *not all there*, and regardless of in which direction we were going, I would have been trying not to understand what the trip meant—that neither of our parents was capable of taking care of us.

I've finally decided that we were on our way to Michigan, to our mother, hoping she'd be waiting when we got there. I would have agreed to anything to get away from Jefferson Junior High School and the townhouse where my father was almost never home. Patti was in Ann Arbor; I don't remember how she got back there but I somehow thought she caught a ride with the Cohens, the nice family that, like ours, still had one foot in Michigan and another in Washington. That might have been the bargain—if I could make the trip with the six- and four-year-old, then my father would let us go back to Ann Arbor and Morningside Drive and U High and our church and my friends. And maybe I wanted to be back with my mother, too.

THE GOOD POETIC MOTHER

Like my false memory that in the fall of 1961 Sara and Ruthie were in Michigan with our mother, and not in the D.C. townhouse with me, Patti, and our father, my account of how that chapter came to an end is contradicted by my mother's recollection. I had always recalled that Patti returned to Michigan first, to join our mother and little sisters, and I do have a clear memory of begging my father to let me go home to Ann Arbor, too. My mother's story, though, was a bit different. More than forty years later, she recalled that "you and Patti didn't like school," and that our father asked her to "take the kids," all of us, back to Michigan. Those confusions seem to connect to the crucial and unanswered question of where exactly our mother was living during those months, which of course really meant whether or not she still was our mother.

Of the following year in Ann Arbor, the last months we spent with her, I have only a disorganized collage of memory—some pieces of 1962 are almost happy, some mystifying, some awful.

I remember a beautiful fall morning when I was up early and Patti was somewhere else and Sara and Ruthie and Mama were still asleep. I had been back in Ann Arbor for at least nine months, had finished eighth grade and started ninth, and either the household hadn't fallen apart yet or I was already exceptionally good at self-delusion. During that year with our mother we had gradually accumulated a menagerie of pets, which we never had before because of our father's allergies. Mama let us have pretty much any kind of animal as long as we promised to take care of it, so besides my parakeet Billy Boy, we had a guinea pig and a couple of kittens and a small black dog. Mama had some strange-but-nice friends up in Jackson (a couple, both psychiatrists, who lived on a small farm and saw patients in their home) who had given us all the animals.

ROUND TWO (MICHIGAN, 1962)

Wearing a pair of not-too-worn-out loafers and knee socks and a pleated wool skirt and a sweater of Patti's that I hoped she wouldn't find out I borrowed, I was going to take the dog for a walk. I tied a length of clothesline to his collar and decided no one could tell it wasn't a real leash. (I think his name might have been Fritzie.) The leaves were turning and I loved how they felt as we crunched through them and how the sky was so high and blue. Even though Fritzie didn't know how to heel and I had to keep starting and stopping, the day was so perfect and the leaves smelled so good and the clothes I was wearing were so right, that I began to believe that I could turn myself into the girl I was pretending to be. I'd walk the dog and keep my clothes clean and maybe do some school activities this year and have nice friends and visit them in their pretty houses near the university.

Maybe Mama wouldn't get too much more unconventional, and Patti—I really didn't know what was going on with Patti. Along with a couple of other eleventh-grade girls, she had started going to Detroit to hang out around Wayne State and go to jazz clubs and flirt with the guys who came to play there. She was still in the school choir, always had a solo at their concerts, and at a talent show had sung "The Silver Swan," which everybody thought was fantastic. Then she'd started taking her guitar to Detroit and sometimes didn't come home until the next day. I tried to stay out of it. Mama was still taking her poetry workshop and the Yevtushenko poem was still painted on the picture window.

In my mother's journal I see that she had already been contemplating how to live on almost nothing a year before this, alone in the Ann Arbor house after our father drove away to Washington with all four girls, but before he came back for Lake Geneva and a last try at reconciliation. She was trying to formulate what grounds she might claim for divorce, figure out if she would have her children with her again, finding a publisher for a newspaper column and some place to live while our house was rented out.

June 24, 1961.

...I still can't think of "grounds." This is going to be very important, because if I don't I'm licked. I'll just have to keep the kids with me and try to think straight.

June 26, 1961.

...I feel at a standstill. I am ready for a new thing but where is it? What is it? Never mind, it will turn up; probably too soon for comfort.

Oh yes—MPF and skimmed-milk powder have to be found if I am to stay healthy cheaply—before Lake Geneva if possible, so I am ready when I get back with the kids. And a cheap source of vitamin C.

Frances Dean Smith (Journal)

I recognized her reference to "MPF" when I read this entry, but it has taken some research to put this strange foodstuff in context. In my own early 1960s experience, "Multipurpose Food" seemed to be something uniquely connected to our incomprehensible mother (Patti said we would someday write a book called *Mama and the MPF*). I know now that this vitamin-enriched soybean product had been developed by a former missionary after World War II, as a solution to both U.S. poverty and world hunger. It was promoted by a foundation called "Meals for Millions," which by the 1950s had enthusiastic supporters among progressive figures like Eleanor Roosevelt, Pearl Buck, and Albert Schweitzer. MPF was advertised as having a "slightly nutty" flavor, was supposed to provide the nutritional equivalent of a full-course meal in each two-ounce serving, and could be eaten cold, hot, or blended with, for example, reconstituted nonfat dry milk. By the1960s, MPF was being promoted for use in fallout shelters.

My mother might have learned about MPF from a variety of sources. What is less clear is why she so readily embraced living on something developed for indigent and starving people? It seems of a piece with the peanut butter crackers and raisins I recall from that days-long train trip when I was four. She mentioned the same crackers in her journal in August 1961, on her way to California to see her mother and sister: "At South Bend, Indiana, in the bus depot for a 30-minute stop, eating cheese-peanut butter crackers. Six cents."

Sometime in the fall of 1962, Mama told me about a civic theater play she thought I should try out for. I didn't know where she got the idea I could do that, except that I'd been in the Thespian Society during the second half of eighth grade. There were going to be tryouts and all I had to do was go over to the local junior high on Monday night and read something from the script. I wasn't sure I could act but I wanted to try to have something about me that people would like.

On Monday night I walked across the field at the end of Morningside Drive to Forsythe Junior High School. There was a sign on the front door that said "A2CT Tryouts in Gymnasium" and I tried to pretend I wasn't scared and followed another sign down the hall to the gym where there were a bunch of adults and no other kids. A man said he was going to direct a play called *The Grass Harp* and he was telling everyone what it was about and no one asked me what I was doing there. When he described the different parts he looked at me when he got to a character named "Verena" and said I might want to "read for that part," whatever that meant. Without really knowing how it happened, by the end of the evening I had the part of Verena and a list of rehearsal dates and the grownups congratulated me and it all seemed pretty wonderful even if it was still confusing.

Mama seemed to be glad about me being in a play, and not as surprised as I was. I hoped this was finally something that would make me stand out. I didn't have to be best at everything the way Patti was, but, if I had just this one thing, I didn't care about still not being in the school choir, and my poem not getting printed in the literary magazine, and my painting never getting chosen for the art show. And maybe Mama would think I was as interesting as Patti was, too.

This next memory is more disturbing. It was maybe late summer or early fall, warm enough so that the living room windows were open. This is important, because those four tall panes, each above a hinged casement, were on the south side of the house, the downhill side, the side toward the neighbors we didn't know very well. We thought they were stuffy, not like Mama's friend Milly on the other side (those two knew a lot about each other and didn't criticize). But there was probably a part of me that wanted to open some windows, wanted somebody to see inside that house, to witness the disorganization that had become chaos and was descending into squalor. It was a reality that I was getting tired of trying to hide and I was starting to not care about consequences.

Mama wasn't there. There was no one in the house except me and a slim young brown-skinned man who I guessed had spent the night. I probably knew his name. I'm not sure now exactly how it went down, but over time I more or less encoded the story like this: "Mama's boyfriend propositioned me and nobody was around and I yelled at him and hoped the neighbors would hear and before anything happened he got scared and left."

What did he really do? Was he talking to me in a suggestive way? Had he been at the party a few weeks earlier, that party where Mama had some man with her, and Patti had a boy down from Detroit, and Patti's boy brought his twenty-one-year old friend, and the friend and I had definitely gotten up to some things I was too young for, that Mama had seen and let pass without comment? Could be. I think he was talking about me and Patti, maybe we were "cool" or "sexy" or "with-it." Perhaps he was feeling me out, seeing the free-for-all that this household had become and wondering how available not only the grown woman but also maybe her two older daughters might be.

The real question is, was I afraid, or was I angry? Angry at him, but mostly at my mother. I have a sick feeling that I set him up, letting him go on talking, all the while poised to start a noisy scene. I started talking back to him, getting louder and louder until he glanced at the windows and told me to keep my voice down.

I didn't keep my voice down. I stood up and shouted, "You better get away from me!" I know I meant to scare him, and it worked. I kept yelling until he ran out the front door. I did want him out of the house, and I didn't know any other way to make that happen. I didn't care then what danger I might have put him in. I didn't care about anybody else.

This memory is really about my mother, not some man, and about the next day. Ordinarily, my mother couldn't get up in the morning. If you wanted to have her in your life, that was just one of the things you had to accept, like the fact that she couldn't, or wouldn't, keep the house clean and organized. You might want to make a fuss, but another thing she couldn't do was abide criticism or complaint, and if you tried any of that she'd get angry or cry, and either way you would end up with even less mother than you had to start with.

But boy, she got up that morning.

I was already out of the house, just starting to walk down the hill toward the bus stop and I heard Mama screaming my name. She ran up behind me, grabbed my shoulder, twisted me around to face her. She was yelling something about the man she was seeing and what I'd said to him, and that she could not believe—and here I remember her words clearly—"that any daughter of mine would be such a racist."

I wrenched away from her while she was still yelling, ran away down the hill, hoping she was standing there crying. We never talked about this again. I've wondered if my outburst cost her that boyfriend, and maybe even back then I felt a tiny bit guilty. Part of me still wanted to be on her side, and another part thought of words like *unwholesome*. I would have known that she didn't care about that; *wholesomeness* was a false idea to her, an arbitrary and restrictive concept meant to keep people locked up in their fears, unable to experience life freely. That's all she was trying to do, to be free, and that's what she thought we should want, too.

Three years later, when I was fifteen and living a life so changed and far from my mother's that it might have been in another dimension, she sent me a twenty-two-page letter, a stream-of-consciousness rant, about societal evils of repression and money, and also quite a lot about sex. She mentioned someone who might have been the man I remember, in a passage about men who are insecure and thus compelled to seduce women. "When we were living in Ann Arbor and I was fairly promiscuous, I did know one man …assuming every un-chaperoned encounter between a man and a woman ends in bed. I was slightly more submissive than I would otherwise be, feeling it necessary to prove that I did like him, worrying vaguely 'he'll think it's because he's a Negro'… which boils down to, for a young woman, or for anyone really, Nuts to seduction."

FOSTER CHILD (MICHIGAN, 1962)

It was not quite the end, but well past the beginning of the end. I remember dark and slush and numb toes and being mad at myself. The child support check wouldn't come for another week, and I'd run out of the share that Mama now handed over to me and Patti, in recognition of her own inability to manage money. I didn't have bus fare and had to walk, again, the two-and-a-half miles from campus to Morningside Drive, dreading the last long straight mile along Miller Road where the wind was always strongest. I tried not to think about my feet; Patti's cast-off black leather boots were unlined and I may not have been wearing socks. The boots were soaked and I was starting to wonder about frostbite. It must have been close to five o'clock when I got to the big evergreen tree that marked the right turn away from Miller, walked that short bit of Pine Tree Drive, turned left on Morningside, and trudged the last two blocks up the hill.

The house was dark.

I let myself in, turned on the light, took off the soggy boots, and warmed my feet on the hot air vent. Then I saw a sheet of lined paper next to a pile of magazines and recognized Mama's handwriting: "I've gone to Detroit to find Patti," she had written.

Patti had begun, weeks earlier, going to Detroit to sing folk music at places with names like the Cup of Socrates and the UnStabled. Then she'd started not coming home for days at a time, and now, I guessed, she was missing.

"Go down to the Hunters' for the night. The little kids are…"

I don't remember where the little kids were. Did she add, "The Hunters are expecting you?" I don't know. I liked the Hunters fine; Mrs. Hunter was a friend of my mother's, Professor Hunter was kind and seemed to genuinely enjoy kids, and they lived just down the block.

My sisters and I were caught at the intersection of our parents' lifelines. Whatever they may have had in common once, his path and hers had begun to diverge some time back and the distance was growing. My father's upwardly-mobile arc had taken him from a trailer park in Arizona to the Army, through a series of technical jobs to an administrative position at the University of Michigan, and now to a senior staff role on a congressional committee. My mother's trajectory seemed to skid in direct opposition, from her grandfather's big house in Lexington, to studying poetry at Smith College, to the WACs and a secretly-essential war job, bottoming out in the worst of a destructive marriage, finding its level in radical self-expression, creative writing, and deliberate barefoot non-conformism.

For the most part staying with the Hunters wasn't bad. Mrs. Hunter was helpful, always worrying that she might not be doing enough for someone else, and didn't mind having one more kid to take to school in the morning. She let my mother set my rules, which meant it was up to me what I did or didn't do. I usually didn't come straight to the Hunters' after school, because I had a boyfriend. Jim and I weren't very happy about most things in our lives—he didn't have a father and his mother drank and he was trying to figure out how to move out and live on his own. We loved each other, though, and thought that money was really our only serious problem. We didn't have any. After school we sometimes walked up to the Michigan Union and sat in one of the lounges until somebody asked us if we were students. That meant university students, and since we weren't, we had to leave. Whenever we had any money at all we went to Dominick's, where we sipped coffee and smelled the pizza. One lucky afternoon the delivery guy dropped a box as he was headed out, and the pizza was smashed. But when the counterman asked if we wanted to have the ruined pie and Jim wasn't too embarrassed to take it, I decided I didn't care. Mangled pizza, no money, living out of a suitcase; I somehow continued to pretend that my life was really okay.

I was always out of cash before the next support check arrived, and one Thursday in the fall of 1962 I didn't have the bus fare to get back to the Hunters' at the end of the day and had to walk again. Mama was supposed to have a check by then, but she was in Detroit and I didn't know how I was supposed to get my share.

When I arrived the others had already had supper, but Mrs. Hunter had saved a plate for me and took it from the oven when I came into the kitchen. "I talked to your mother this afternoon," she said with a smile. "I understand you need to get your allowance this weekend?" I was relieved to hear somebody had a plan for the money. "But she isn't going to be back until next week. I guess she has a poetry class on Tuesday and she'll get a ride then." Mrs. Hunter looked worried. "Fran said I should ask if you want to wait until Tuesday or if you might want to take the bus up to Detroit after school tomorrow and meet up with her there?"

I didn't think she would have allowed one of her own teenagers to go Detroit alone, but she never criticized my mother's choices. I hated taking the bus anywhere, even in Ann Arbor, but I really needed to get some money and maybe I'd like to see Mama and Patti too. But how was I going to pay for the bus?

Mrs. Hunter had the solution even before I had really faced the problem. "Why don't I give you five dollars now, and you can pay me back on the weekend? That should be more than enough for the bus fare, I think."

I hoped that was right. Then I'd be able to buy some lunch on Friday, and if I could get Jim to go with me I wouldn't be so apprehensive about taking the Greyhound all the way to the city. I knew how to get to the theater-coffeehouse where Mama would be, but the bus station and the surrounding neighborhood made me nervous, even though Mama said that was ridiculous.

Jim was waiting for me after school on Friday and liked the idea of going to Detroit. He had his guitar with him, and hoped maybe he'd have a chance to play between sets at the coffeehouse, so we walked the ten blocks to the Ann Arbor bus depot and found a bus leaving for Detroit at five. The tickets were two dollars each; I still had four dollars and some change left from what I borrowed from Mrs. Hunter, and I wasn't worried because as soon as we got to the UnStabled and found Mama I would have plenty of money. For a while at least.

As the bus headed out Plymouth Road toward the freeway in the late-afternoon twilight, light snow blew across the highway. Riding the bus with Jim was completely different from the Greyhound trip I'd made last winter, with two little girls and with not much money then, either. That bus had been awful, worse than the home I'd just left and the one where I hoped to arrive safely. Now it was the bus itself that seemed a safe haven, a respite from being a nervous guest in the Hunters' house; the ninety-minute trip was a reassuring interlude before having to tackle Detroit. And my mother.

Mama had been in Detroit more than at home for weeks, and I couldn't remember the last time Patti had been in our house or at school. I'd come to the coffeehouse once before when Mama brought me and Sara to hear Patti sing, but now I didn't know where Patti was staying or what her plans were, or if she was ever going to come home again. Sometimes it seemed that Mama was thinking of moving to Detroit herself, but there seemed to be a lot missing from that plan, if it was one.

By the time we arrived at the Howard Street bus station, the snow was picking up. We stood outside the depot door and I got my bearings, remembering that we needed to turn right, then left up Third Street. I was sure about that part because it was away from the river, which meant the wind would be at our backs. I didn't have any gloves, but I put one hand in my pocket and held Jim's hand with the other.

I remembered to turn again when we got to Cass, and hoped I'd recognize the right cross street. It was getting even colder but I thought about the cocoa or coffee we could get when we made it to the theater, and was still excited with our adventure. Finally, we turned on Temple Street and I could see the UnStabled in the next block. I realized that I hadn't been completely sure about finding our way, and shivered either from relief or cold. I couldn't wait to get inside.

A tall man, dressed in jeans and a Wayne State sweatshirt, was sitting on a stool just inside the door, smoking and reading a newspaper. I didn't recognize him, but he smiled at us. "No cover tonight, folks," he said. "The theater's dark and we don't have anyone coming to do folk music. There'll be some jazz later on if you want to stay that long."

THE GOOD POETIC MOTHER

Jim and I looked at each other, and then around the low-ceilinged room. I didn't see Mama, or Patti, or anyone I knew. The jukebox was playing soft jazz. Two men were hunched over a chess board, a younger man was taking notes from a textbook, and a woman sitting alone—not Mama—was reading a magazine and drinking coffee and smoking.

"Nobody's singing tonight?" I asked, even though he'd already said there wouldn't be any folk music.

"Not tonight. But you folks are welcome to come on in and have some coffee or tea or something. It's getting awful cold out there." Jim and I looked at each other.

"Maybe my mother will still come even though Patti's not going to sing," I whispered. "Do we have enough money to get anything?" Jim pulled out a handful of change.

"Maybe if we share. Cocoa or cider?"

"It's your money, you choose." Anything would be fine with me and I was feeling shaky again. I kept looking at one table after another, as if one of these strangers might magically turn into my mother.

I don't know how long we waited before we had to face the fact that she wasn't coming. I had no idea where Patti was living or where Mama stayed when she didn't sit at the coffeehouse all night, and I was afraid Jim would be mad at me. Of course he wasn't, but he was worried. We didn't have enough money to get anything to eat, we didn't have a place to stay, and we didn't have the bus fare back. Then I remembered that I had told Mrs. Hunter that we'd get the 9:20 bus, and that she had said Professor Hunter would pick us up when it got in at eleven. Somehow the thought of being in trouble with her, and with Professor Hunter, was worse than everything else put together. I turned away from Jim, put my hands over my mouth and closed my eyes.

"Come on, it's not that bad. We'll figure out something. You have the Hunters' phone number, right? They've got pay phones at the bus station. Maybe somebody can come and get us." Jim put his arm around me and I felt less shaky. We got our jackets and his gloves and he picked up his guitar, and we headed back out into the night. On Third Street the wind off the river was right in our faces and the last ten blocks seemed longer than they had been on the way over. We held on to each other, teeth chattering.

Finally, we saw the lights of the bus station, and then we were stumbling through the revolving door. The waiting room was warm and bright and not quite as busy as when we were there earlier, and we sat down on one of the wooden benches to catch our breath. Then Jim found the pay phones, and gave me his last dime. I dialed the Hunters' number, crossing my fingers that somebody (and not one of the kids, because I didn't want them to know I badly I messed this up) would be home.

Mrs. Hunter answered and somehow I explained to her what had happened. I was trying to sound grown up and responsible, but my voice was shaking.

"Oh, dear. I was afraid this wasn't a good idea, but your mother said—well, we'll figure something out. Where are you now? Is Jim with you?"

"We came back to the bus station, but I don't have any money to pay our way back and Jim's out of money too." I had to stop talking because I was crying again.

"Well, let me think. I don't have the car because Bob is working late. So I can't drive up there to get you. Is there somebody from the bus company there? Why don't you see if I can talk to one of the Greyhound people?"

THE GOOD POETIC MOTHER

I asked Jim to find somebody to help us—he had all the self-confidence with strangers that I lacked, and went directly to the ticket counter, returning in a couple of minutes with a short, fat, gray-haired man wearing a navy blue jacket with a Greyhound patch and name tag, and a hat pushed to the back of his head. "Who am I going to talk to now? Your mother?" he asked me.

"No, she's a neighbor, but I'm staying with them and we forgot our money to get back to Ann Arbor and—" The man nodded and took the receiver from me and waved for me and Jim to go sit down again. He talked for a minute or two and we couldn't hear all of it but finally he said, "Okay, then. I'll take care of it on this end. And somebody will be at the station in Ann Arbor? Right. He can just pay the driver. That'll work fine. No problem, glad to help."

Professor Hunter would pay for our tickets when the bus arrived in Ann Arbor and then he'd drop Jim off at his mother's and then take me home with him. The bus station man wasn't mad at us and Mrs. Hunter didn't seem to be too upset and maybe when I got back there would be some dinner left.

Maybe it was the Detroit debacle that made the Hunters feel it was time for me to move on to another family.

I arrived at the Webers' house on a Saturday morning, and Mrs. Weber showed me the guest room and the bathroom. "You'll want to freshen up, dear." She glanced at my tiny vinyl suitcase. "Do you need a toothbrush?" Of course I did, and she brought me one still in its package. Above her unchanging lipsticked smile, sharp dark eyes scrutinized me. We were close enough for me to notice powder caked in fine lines around her eyes and mouth and some gray at the roots of her spray-stiff auburn curls.

Patti was still in Detroit, Mama still working out what to do about it, and most of the time no one was actually at our house. Sara and

FOSTER CHILD (MICHIGAN, 1962)

Ruthie were, I thought, with our next-door neighbor, but I had to stay with somebody who went to the University School, whose parents could give me a ride to school. Somebody like Andy Weber. Blond crew cut, pressed chinos, in ninth grade like me. In some self-deluding fantasy state, I'd hoped he'd notice me, maybe even like me.

I would have to ask her. "Do you have any, um, sanitary supplies? Because I forgot…"

Mrs. Weber brought me an unopened box of Kotex. "Just us girls," she smiled. I slumped away from her, ducked behind limp hair, eyes hot with relief and embarrassment. But she was still talking. "I hope you didn't have an accident, dear. That's why I always have dark underwear for that time of the month. It's so hard to get those stains out."

I try to imagine what would have happened if I'd been able to let her in right then, told her that I didn't have white underpants for some days and colored ones for others, had only the pair I was wearing, just like the jumper and blouse I had on were the only clothes that still fit. Then I might have said I wanted to stay with her forever, that I needed somebody to buy me some clothes, starting with underwear, maybe even the set of seven lace-trimmed panties I'd yearned for in grade school, a rainbow of pastels with the day of the week embroidered at the hip.

It would have taken far more than underwear, of course, more than getting down to the skin, to make myself right; deeper than that to clean away the self-loathing that was becoming part of my core.

Mrs. Weber was going to take me to get my hair cut that afternoon, and she asked pointedly if I preferred to take a bath or a shower. "Out of consideration for the hairdresser, dear. Otherwise I wouldn't say anything, but I've noticed a little B.O. You want to be clean and fresh for the hairdresser, don't you?"

Perhaps because I hadn't answered her yet and she thought my silence meant defiance, she went on. "And some deodorant, dear. Because I don't like to tell you this, but Andy noticed, too. He mentioned it to his father and me. The B.O., I mean."

It could have been any one of the other mothers who'd been taking me in and probably getting tired of it. These weeks of cycling through other people's houses run together in my memory, and the only thing I remember clearly is my humiliation, her kindness—and how much I hated her.

SUNDAY SCHOOL (MICHIGAN, 1962)

"A man's got responsibilities," I heard a man say.

He was talking about my father. I was standing in the hallway outside the Unitarian church office, between the mansion that once *was* the church, and the modern stone-and-glass addition, with its airy sanctuary and the spacious basement for the coffee hour that always seemed such an essential part of being Unitarian. I could remember when we first joined, just arrived in Michigan from California in 1955, when services had been held in a sunny side porch, Sunday school classes in various bedrooms, and the children roamed the back stairs and passages of the old house, discovering unknown rooms, having exciting yet safe adventures.

I'm not sure how I got to church that day. My mother had gradually lost her hold on this affiliation, as she had let so much slip away that year. There had been a time when she wrote for the church newsletter, my father headed up committees, she started and kept up with a young couples' club, and we were part of an extended community that always felt to me like a second (and better) family. I tried to get to church when I could.

It must have been after the service and before coffee hour, and I might have been on my way to youth group. I remember three things for sure:

What I was wearing: a dress that belonged to my mother—ecru cotton, with a stylized paisley print in navy blue or black, fitted waist, full skirt, wide boat neck. A lovely dress, and in no way appropriate for a fourteen-year-old girl. When my mother had worn this dress she had been pretty and engaged and people liked her and didn't think she was crazy, and maybe I hoped it would work that way for me, too. I pushed away the fear that I really seemed an overgrown child playing dress-up. Why was I wearing my mother's dress? I'm sure now that it was an attempt to solve the problem of having almost no clothes of my own.

What I was doing: standing at the bulletin board, looking at one particular newspaper clipping among other announcements and flyers. I saw a photograph of my father—handsome, smiling—heading an article from the *Ann Arbor News*. It said he'd taken a year's leave from the University of Michigan to be the Education Chief of the Committee on Education and Labor of the U.S. House of Representatives. I would not have understood much of that (I had thought at first that he would be working at the White House). Why was I looking at this article, definitely not for the first time? I was showing off, wanting attention, hoping to be noticed. Wishing someone might remember that I was one of his daughters, and that they admired him and liked me. I hoped that, despite the tattered reality of my home life with a single parent, I might claim some of the status and respectability conferred by the other, the one who was so far away.

SUNDAY SCHOOL (MICHIGAN, 1962)

What I heard: a man speaking behind me, not to me, but in conversation with other adults. I don't know if I realized at first that they were talking about my father, but now suspect that I *did* understand that, and that would have been precisely why I lingered at the bulletin board. I might have hoped to hear something like, "impressive opportunity for him… going to do great things down there… a smart guy." And then they would notice me. "There's one of his daughters. Amazing how they all look like him, four blue-eyed blondes. Bright girls, too." My hopeful fantasy would have run along those lines.

That wasn't what the man was saying at all.

"It's one thing if a man can't get along with his wife… ignoring this mess up here… out of control… off her rocker… he needs to deal with it. A man's got responsibilities."

What happened next? I'm sure I tried to slip away, as if in a hurry to go to youth group and not really interested in the bulletin board. What did I think? I was searingly embarrassed, hated the man I'd overheard, ashamed both of the reality of my life and of my stupid delusion that it could somehow still be seen otherwise, that I myself could be worthy of some esteem instead of pity and disdain.

Only much later could I remember this incident with less personal shame and with some sense of validation. Things *were* a mess, regardless of whether that was my mother's fault or my father's, and we desperately needed someone to step in and make things right. I have wondered, too, if what I overheard was evidence of a larger discussion, if there were people in Ann Arbor, perhaps former friends of my parents, who had noted and discussed what was happening in the house on Morningside Drive. Our mother was on her own, getting child support checks (not enough) and trying to manage the four of us (not well) and the household was in an accelerating downhill slide.

If the adults I overheard that Sunday had been talking about us, and if someone had actually gotten in touch with my father to remind him of his responsibilities, he would have been furious. He wanted to be seen as a man capable of taking charge of anything, and would have had to do something to prop up that image. He would be the good one, and she would have to be the bad one, whatever it took.

SHE'S HAD IT (MICHIGAN, 1962)

"I've had it with her! You have to take her, that's all. I mean it. I can't put up with it and I'm not going to!" My mother was on the phone, calling my father in Washington. And I was trying to figure out what had just happened.

I'd woken up maybe thirty minutes earlier, to dim blue light coming through the uncurtained window of my half-basement bedroom, and heard Mama's footsteps above. I wiggled out of the sleeping bag that, on top of an old box spring, had been my bed since I came back from D.C. almost a year earlier, when I'd been thirteen and a half and still hoped that living with my mother in Ann Arbor was something that might work out. I still thought it was better than moping around my father's empty townhouse, but it was definitely not working out.

The tights I wore under my nightgown were footless, a relic of some long-ago modern dance class, and I hopped to the closet to shove my bare feet into scuffed brown loafers. The gray vinyl tiles were laid directly on a concrete slab, and in the winter the floor made my feet ache. Frost ferns bloomed from each corner of the window glass, and the plasterboard ledge under the window was spongy, with gray spots that seemed to have spread since winter began. Outside, a foot or so below the window, was patchy snow, frozen mud, and dead grass.

The light on the red-and-white RCA record player glowed dimly, reminding me to turn the turntable off. The suitcase-style portable was not exactly mine—if Patti ever came home again she might have decided it was hers, or Mama might have wanted to take it back upstairs, but for the moment it was my most precious possession. As I touched the knob, a buzzing shock ran through my fingers and arm, up to the elbow. I was angry at the record player for a second, but I knew it was my fault. I needed to take better care of it, find a box or a table to get it off the basement floor. I hoped it wasn't really dangerous.

I needed that record player, a necessary prop to support my escape to a fantasy of a better, or at least less terrible, life. With music, I could almost convince myself that my family was not so radically changed, or perhaps could still be restored to the period of calm and stability that had existed a year and a half earlier. We used to have more records—brittle and heavy 78s (*Peter and the Wolf*, Alan Lomax, Nichols and May comedy routines) and newer 33s (*South Pacific*, the Weavers, Kingston Trio). Mama didn't listen to them now, and I hadn't seen them in a long time. Maybe they had been packed the summer before last, when we had all been supposed to move to D.C. but instead Mama decided she wanted a divorce and my sisters and I went with Daddy for a few grim months and then left him and came back here. Now I had one record, and when I was actually in my own house, I played Tchaikovsky's First Piano Concerto after I turned out the light. It helped me go to sleep, took me away to an imagined better existence, where people listened to classical music and had food in the cupboards and actual beds and two parents.

SHE'S HAD IT (MICHIGAN, 1962)

I found my glasses on the floor next to the mattress, and rummaged under the sleeping bag for Patti's old green sweatshirt. I didn't know what Patti might do if she caught me wearing it, but I didn't have anything else and besides, she wasn't there. I remembered when she'd brought this trophy back from a youth group trip to Benton Harbor. Someone had written on the back with a felt-tipped marker, in big curvy letters, "Wanna neck?" and in smaller letters underneath, "Sorry, it's mine."

At the bathroom mirror, I pushed my hair behind my ears. I couldn't find my hairbrush, or a toothbrush. We didn't have any toothpaste, because Mama said you can rub baking soda on your teeth and gums and it does just as good a job and it's too bad so many people think they have to spend money on stuff like that—but we didn't have any baking soda either.

I hoped there might be some oatmeal, and not just the crumbly light-brown granules of Multipurpose Food that Mama started ordering by mail sometime after she ended up back here in Michigan, trying to stretch the child support checks and being, as she always had been, even worse at managing money than she was at keeping house. I found the MPF so completely disgusting that I couldn't make myself eat it, even to show some solidarity with Mama. Mama had given up trying to force it on Patti and me, but that didn't mean she always had something else.

She'd been in a bad mood since she came back from Detroit and Patti didn't. Not the staying-in-bed-all-day kind of depressed, but clearly not happy, and mad at somebody. I'd make my oatmeal and stay out of her way.

The little kids must have still been asleep. They had one of the two front bedrooms, Patti had the other, and Mama slept on a mattress in an alcove off the living room. She said a mattress on the floor was perfectly adequate, and that it was silly to think there had to be a frame or a headboard.

Even before I saw Mama, I was annoyed with her, for no particular reason. And for every reason. She was wearing a rumpled denim skirt and gray cardigan, over the faded red shirt from her days in the WACs, and her curly dark hair was standing up in the back. What surprised me was not what a mess she looked, but that she seemed to be mad at me, too.

"Is there any oatmeal left?" I asked her. I didn't see it on the counter.

"Well, I'm sure I don't know," she snapped. "And who was your servant this time last week?" We'd never had servants, of course, but this was a familiar phrase. She was the one who'd grown up with a maid and a housekeeper and a cook, back in her grandfather's house in Massachusetts. She had a fancy New England family once, and while she never wanted to talk about it, and of course it was sad that her father died when she was so young, I had always imagined that life as one I'd have given anything for. (She even went, for a while at least, to a college I was just starting to understand meant something, and the other title Patti suggested for our book was *Mama Went to Smith*.)

This who-was-your-servant line was kind of a joke, like, "That's the upstairs maid's job," but this morning she was just being snotty.

"I just asked if we have any. I didn't mean you should get it for me." I wasn't mouthing off, but trying to explain, to placate her. I edged around her, wanting to get to the kitchen. She was following me, and I could tell she had more to say. It was like she was in the middle of a fight with somebody else.

"Apparently I'm supposed to be keeping you girls on a shorter leash, did you know that? And how am I expected to do that without

SHE'S HAD IT (MICHIGAN, 1962)

any help, when you won't even come home at night?" She sounded both angry and close to tears. She took a long drag from her cigarette. "Things are going to have to shape up around here, you better realize that!" Not so shaky, gathering strength. Whoever else she'd been mad at before, it was just me now. "Do you even know what a curfew is? I've had it with you coming and going whenever you want! You think you can stay out with your supposed boyfriend whenever you feel like it. Well, you've got another think coming!"

"Another think coming" was Daddy's phrase. It meant trouble.

"And what are you doing with a boyfriend, anyway?" She was getting louder. "You're fourteen fucking years old. This is ridiculous, and it's going to stop, do you hear me?"

I did know what a curfew was—it was something other people's families had and we didn't, because Mama thought rules were conformist and unnecessary, because of course parents should treat kids with respect and expect them to take responsibility for themselves. And why was a boyfriend a bad thing all of a sudden? She seemed to like Patti's boyfriends just fine. She'd had boyfriends herself, brought them here plenty of times, and that was a whole other bad story. As for not coming home at whatever the right time was supposed to be, what about the time when I got up one night and Mama wasn't even in the house? She hadn't come back until the sun was coming up, and I had stayed awake, curled up on her bed wrapped in her shawl, trying not to think about what would happen to us if she never returned. When she did finally get home, I went back to my room and neither of us ever said anything about it.

Or how about when she first started chasing Patti to Detroit and forgetting about the rest of us, and the day I came home from school one afternoon to find that note that started the nomadic period of

THE GOOD POETIC MOTHER

staying with other people more than in my own house and never being quite sure where my mother or any of my sisters were?

"Do you know anything about anything?" she shouted. "You'd better shape up pretty soon if you want to stay in my house!" And now she sounded even more like Daddy. If it had been one of their fights, the yelling would have gone back and forth for however many rounds it took to make her cry.

"I was home by ten!" I protested. "Since when is that supposed to be too late? And I don't see Patti coming home any earlier, I don't see her coming home at all!" I was on dangerous ground, but couldn't stop. "How come you're yelling at me and you let her get away with anything she wants to?"

She wasn't having it.

"I'm your mother and you're the child and you can't tell me what to do!" I was surprised neither of my little sisters had woken up, started to cry, created a diversion. "You're not doing your job around here. I'm sick of you and your attitude. You think you're so smart but you know what? You don't know anything. Anything about anything." She'd said that already. So had Daddy. I didn't know anything, I was stupid, I didn't do my job.

And then I said what I'd been wanting to say all morning, all this month, probably all year. "Well." I stopped for a moment. "I know one thing." She squinted at me.

"I know you're not a very good mother."

My voice was quiet, but I was looking straight at her. She might have hit me at this point, but I guess I was willing for that to happen.

We were standing perhaps four feet apart. She had a coffee mug in one hand, a cigarette in the other. Maybe that's why she didn't slap me right away. She didn't slap me at all, but stared at me, a cold stare that

SHE'S HAD IT (MICHIGAN, 1962)

seemed to last for minutes. "Fine. I'm not a good mother. Fine. That's it." She turned away, took three strides to the kitchen, grabbed the receiver from the wall phone, and punched in a long-distance number.

GOODBYE TO ALL THAT (MICHIGAN, 1962)

"I think we should just break up," I blurted. Jim's friendly face clouded with confusion and disbelief, and he opened his mouth as if to say something. I went on before he could speak, ignoring what seemed to be the beginning of tears in his eyes. "Because, obviously, we're going to have to say goodbye anyway, so let's just do it now." I'm sure I felt there was some kind of logic to this. I didn't wait to say goodbye, but turned and walked away, leaving him standing alone.

I remember where we were—on Arch Street, not far from the University of Michigan's Ferry Field track, perhaps right in front of the Adams' Dutch colonial house—which means that I was staying not in my own house on Morningside Drive (I knew Mama wasn't there either, although not where she'd gone), or down the hill with the Hunters, and not with the Webers, but, for this last time, with my old friend Sally's family.

For months Jim had been the only person in my life who cared about me, and I was about to break his heart. I'd given him the news that my mother was gone, that I was going to be sent to my father in Washington, and that at least some of my sisters were, too. I didn't know exactly when this would happen but maybe I needed to take control of some part of the whole catastrophe. I was about to transfer my life and loyalty from one parent to the other, and while there would eventually be many things about my father that I would emulate and later regret, this was the worst thing I copied from my mother. I would be the one to leave, and someone, at least, would know how I felt.

The following year, when she was living in a rooming house in Los Angeles, my mother wrote a poem that seems to summarize her understanding of what happened in our final year together:

> KEEPING HOUSE III
> *So the wanderer leaves*
> *his nest in the care of*
> *the one at home.*
> *A mistake. She can't care*
> *for the nest*
> *without*
> *the builder.*
>
> *Out the window with you,*
> *dog, cat, canary, and crockery.*
> *Nobody wants you now,*
> *poor*
> *children.*
>
> S. S. Veri (aka Frances Dean Smith), 1964

On Friday I went to school as usual, and that morning had walked the five blocks to the university women's pool with the other ninth-grade girls for our weekly swimming class. The lesson was over, limp cotton tank suits thrown into the rolling canvas bin, school clothes retrieved from lockers, and everyone but me putting on their coats. Perhaps I didn't quite let myself know that it was my last day in Ann Arbor, last swimming lesson, last hour with my classmates. The others certainly didn't realize anything was different, only that I had to stay behind when they left to walk back to school, because someone would be picking me up to go—somewhere.

I'd hoped to stay in Ann Arbor at least until the end of the term, maybe leave at the start of Christmas break, but that's not how it had worked out. I looked out the floor-to-ceiling windows to the courtyard, the slope up to the street, landscaped with ivy and evergreen shrubs, and waited. Alone in the lobby, I could hear echoes from the pool—coaches shouting, diving board thumping, divers splashing. The chlorine smell wasn't as sharp out here, but my eyes were still sore from the treated water and the overhead lights were surrounded by iridescent halos. I used to think that was beautiful.

I remembered coming to this pool for Wednesday family swim nights when we were first in Michigan—me and Mama and Patti and baby Sara. Once Mama brought me here to see synchronized swimming. I was entranced, found it achingly beautiful, longed with a hopeless passion to be one of those graceful fish-like young women. Now I knew I wouldn't see the haloed lights again, wouldn't walk the blocks from the pool back to school to sit in science class with frozen strands of hair clicking against the back of my chair. What I didn't know is where my mother was or how things had come apart so completely.

Had the unravelling actually begun a few weeks earlier? In October I'd overheard Mama talking about the divorce hearing. She'd been pacing the kitchen, tethered by a long yellow coil of telephone cord, sarcastic and angry, but also close to tears. "Yeah, it's over. I know I should be glad. But that goddamned judge..." I don't think she was talking to me, but I can't remember anyone else there. That's why I have to imagine the telephone, because otherwise it would mean she'd been talking to herself. The judge had said, in open court, "Well, I will grant the—*cough, cough*—'lady'—*cough*—her divorce."

Why his contempt? Certainly my mother's life had become more and more unconventional since she and my father separated, but how could the judge know about the lovers, the filthy house, the feral children? Maybe it was her appearance—did she wear sandals to court? Any shoes at all? But I was mad, too, hearing how she'd been mocked. *That goddamned judge*, I thought. I was still on Mama's side.

I had still been on her side in early November, on the day my homeroom teacher caught up with me outside school. Mrs. Cook, in her shirtwaist dress and coordinated cardigan, was pretending to care about me. Her lips were curved in a smile that did not extend to her ever-appraising eyes, and she said, in a confiding tone I'd never heard before, "I understand that you'll be going back to Washington, dear."

Did I understand that yet?

"I'm sorry to hear you have to leave, of course, but I'm sure you know that your mother is mentally ill. It's really wonderful of your father to take you all in, I must say. I hope you appreciate that, dear. And I just wanted to tell you that if you want to talk about any of this, you can come to me."

No, I didn't actually know my mother was mentally ill. My parents called each other crazy in almost every fight, but I thought my mother was at least as sane as my father. I just knew that I hated Mrs. Cook and would never talk to her about my mother or anything else.

Waiting at the pool I realized that I wouldn't see her again, wouldn't have to listen to her judgment on the unanswerable question of which parent was right and which was wrong, who was crazy and who was sane. I did wonder, though, if she might know where my mother had gone.

UP ON THE ROOF (WASHINGTON, 1963)

The girl let the apartment door close behind her. She was fourteen now, far from being a child but not close to being the woman she (and her mother) had been pretending she was for the previous year. Down the hall to the elevators. She didn't push the arrow pointing down, as she would if she'd wanted to descend four floors to the apartment house lobby and front doors and perhaps take a walk, if she had anywhere to go. She chose the up-arrow instead, rose four more floors to the eighth. Down another hall, pulling open a heavy door, climbing metal steps to an even heavier door, this one steel. Then outside in the sunshine, bare feet on red terracotta tiles. There were no patio chairs or lounges or tables, just a chain-link fence surrounding the tiled area, a flat roof encrusted with white pebbles beyond the fence.

The girl I was had no words at the time to describe this chapter of her life. Even if she had, there was no one to speak to, to help her understand what had happened and what it was going to mean. She might as well sit on the edge of the roof of the apartment building, looking across the city where she now lived; it seemed as reasonable as anything else in her life. She was alone, didn't know where her mother was, soon would not know where her older sister had gone, either. Her father was seldom present, and, worst of all, she didn't really know where her little sisters were much of the time, and she was supposed to be in charge of them. Her life had undergone a radical discontinuity, shocking her into a kind of stasis in which she couldn't talk or think. The woman I am now still has trouble finding the narrative thread.

"Shock" comes directly from the French verb *choquer*, describing a military maneuver of charging directly at troops in order to throw them into confused disarray. Physical shock is a potentially fatal condition characterized by insufficient blood pressure; untreated it may lead rapidly to organ failure. (Psychogenic shock can result in syncope, or fainting, which resolves once adequate blood flow to the brain is restored; collapse is in that case the cure.)

The girl's sense of what led to what, the unfolding of this chapter of her life, was lost. Procedural memory would be spared; she still knew who she was, and if she'd had a bicycle she'd have been able to ride it. Almost the last thing the girl remembered clearly was the day her mother told her she had to go. Whatever had happened right before that was unclear, as was much of what happened next.

My persistent amnesia, like the aftereffects of concussion, extends backward and forward. Both retrograde and anterograde amnesia may result from a blow that prevents experiences, having registered in short-term memory immediately before or just after the injury, from being encoded to long-term recall. (Narrative memory is the primary casualty.)

My recall of the months after arriving back in Washington at the end of 1962 is as hazy as my understanding of the final weeks in

UP ON THE ROOF (WASHINGTON, 1963)

Michigan. I know where I was and know who must have been there (800 Fourth Street, SW, Washington, D.C.; myself and, for a time at least, all three of my sisters. It was our father's apartment, but his presence seems shadowy or shadowed.)

"Amnesia" is Greek, meaning forgetfulness, and "amnesty" is one of its direct descendants, showing that it entails forgetting more than forgiving. People ask me if I have forgiven my mother, and the question seems irrelevant. Amnesty might have been the best we could hope for.

The girl always remembered the incident of the dress code but I do not know for sure, having decided and changed my mind more than once, when that actually occurred. It might have been in the fall of 1961, when the girl encountered the hated school for the first time and was still able to record the event in long-term memory. But it might have been this second and final spell in Washington, at the end of 1962 and beginning of 1963, an exception to the pervasive fog of those months. All she had, and all I have, to fix that memory is an item of clothing.

In later memory, the apartment always seemed to be empty. Alone, she heard the classical radio station sign off for the evening with a hymn (I can still recall the melody and a few of the words). Probably the little girls were there, asleep. The oldest girl was already gone for good, their father not coming home that night, their mother not coming home ever.

"Bleak" as an adjective means, "barren, exposed to the elements." It can signify the absence of hope, or a situation not likely to have a favorable outcome. It comes from Old English and Old Norse *blac*, meaning "shining white" and related to "bleach," as in bleached bones, for example.

She wandered—to a nearby drugstore, with no money and nothing to buy. Sometimes north four blocks to the grassy Mall, the National

Gallery of Art, barefoot on cool marble floors. At least once to the roof of the eight-story apartment building, over the chain link that enclosed a terrace. She sat down at the corner of the building, her right foot dangling above G Street, the left foot over Fourth, the Capitol to her right, the Washington Monument to her left.

I have no idea what she was thinking.

Wandering is a characteristic of psychogenic fugue, a psychiatric state involving depersonalization, derealization, and pervasive amnesia. It is not clear to me how much that girl knew where and who she was, if she could remember who she'd been or imagine who she might become.

We lived in that apartment with my father for perhaps eight months. I don't know if I had finished the first semester of ninth grade before leaving Michigan, if I returned to the D.C. school at the start of second semester or weeks before, or if it would have made any difference. I can't recall much about being at school; even less about what I did when, as often, I didn't go to school at all.

That school, of course, wasn't the sole or even primary source of suffering. Life had been unraveling for some time before I returned the final time to Washington, but the harsh experiences there represented how terrible the world was going to be, and my recollection of the school came to contain the entire constellation of unmanageable and unbearable reality.

The word "grief" is unchanged from Middle English, rooted in Old French *grever*, meaning "burden or encumber." Something serious or severe, in English, may be characterized as "grave," from Old French *greve*, for something terrible or dreadful. "Grave" as a place of burial comes from Old English *graef*, and this is the meaning in "engrave," something that has been dug into a surface, leaving a permanent mark.

DERELICTION OF DUTY (WASHINGTON, 1963)

A few weeks after sending his daughters and soon-to-be ex-wife from D.C. back to Ann Arbor in late 1961, our father moved on from the congressional committee that had brought him to Washington and took a position at the newly-founded Peace Corps. He worked for President Kennedy's brother-in-law, Sargent Shriver, was in charge of training programs for volunteers in South America, and for most of July had been out of town—first in Texas, then Oklahoma, and now Brazil. He wouldn't be home for my fifteenth birthday at the end of the month.

By this point I'd given up hoping my own life would be better because of our father's accomplishments—he had the right kind of job, but we still weren't the right kind of family. We weren't really a family at all. I had once imagined that our father's success might elevate the status of all of us, and for a brief time when we were first back in D.C. for the third round of custody, it seemed to be working out that way for Patti. After round two, in Ann Arbor with our mother, and then running away to Detroit and being arrested, and then being in D.C.

THE GOOD POETIC MOTHER

again, she didn't return to public school. Instead she was enrolled at a private, progressive school housed in a three-story brownstone a block from Dupont Circle. The father of one of her classmates worked at the White House—our father knew what a *Science Advisor* was and Patti's friend seemed to know what being a *Deputy Associate Director* meant. People paid attention to Patti, and she could have been on her way to being one of the cool kids. She was there for five months before she ran away again.

It was sometime in May, two months after her seventeenth birthday, and even after all the times she'd left Ann Arbor for Detroit the year before, this disappearance took me by surprise. I'd thought that because she'd joined the rest of us in D.C., seemed to like her school and her friends, and didn't have to deal with our mother, she'd stay. Now I was starting to realize that neither of them would be coming home.

After a couple of weeks, someone (not my father) told me Patti had been picked up by the police and was being held at a place called Junior Village. That was where kids had to go if they were troubled, or in trouble, or both. I learned that Patti was pregnant, and later I would find out that she was with our mother again, this time in California. Both of them were staying with Grandma Dean in Garden Grove. I wondered if Patti didn't want to return to our father's apartment, or if he'd refused to let her; if Grandma Dean had sent a plane ticket, or if he'd paid for it. All I knew was that she was gone.

When his ex-wife and daughters had been back in Michigan for nine months, our father moved out of the family-ready townhouse and into a "junior one-bedroom" in a high-rise building. It had been perfect for the bachelor my father had been, and that he probably hoped to continue being. It was not perfect for an adult man and four girls, five to sixteen, and not much better even after the eldest daughter left. There was one actual bedroom and another smaller room separated from the living room by an accordion door. I can see the vertical blinds and dark parquet floor, have an idea that the kitchen was really part of the living room, and know that there was a narrow balcony overlooking Fourth Street. I didn't then, and don't now, have a clear sense of who was where.

What did the younger girls do all day? They must have had some toys, or books, or games. Did A. A. Milne make the trip from Ann Arbor? What about their Raggedy Ann dolls? And what did I do? I had survived my childhood by spending hours immersed in books, but I can't remember having anything to read in that apartment and I can't imagine how I managed without that escape.

I did have my guitar. That was one of the most important things Nanny had done for me—she understood that I wanted a guitar like the one Patti had taken with her when she left, and, having convinced my father to pay for it, took me on a birthday outing to a pawn shop in Rosslyn, Virginia. I still have that guitar.

After Patti left, her boyfriend Jon—along with a rotation of other boys (never any girls) who had followed her around—stopped coming over to the apartment. But Lucky, Jon's sidekick and oldest friend, still sometimes biked down to "New Southwest" from Northwest D.C. where he lived with his mother. His high, clear whistle as he turned on to Fourth Street—almost always Lead Belly's "Down and Out"—gave me a rush of excitement, awakening me from what I can now see was a chronic state of hopeless paralysis.

Lucky was almost eighteen, although he was not much taller than I and seemed younger than his friend Jon. I don't think it was his height that made him seem closer to my own age, but his soft brown eyes and open friendliness—unlike Patti's other friends he never seemed to be trying to show how cool he was. I wished he were my boyfriend, of course; but just having someone to spend time with, to teach me some guitar chords, someone kind, was enough.

I still remember the afternoon he dropped by the apartment sometime between lunch and supper. Sara and Ruthie were excited to have company, too, but they had been bored all afternoon and now were hungry. "Can we have some cereal?" Sara got Ruthie to ask me, maybe because she knew I'd be more patient with the five-year-old than with her. But I couldn't give them what they wanted.

"I'm sorry, honey, but we're out of milk. Can't you wait until suppertime?" There had been someone during that period who came to fix dinner for us at least some of the time, but I can't reconstruct now what food there might have been in the apartment, or why I was so unable to figure out how to get the little ones a snack.

Lucky opened the refrigerator, closed it, and frowned. "I'll be back." I didn't know where he'd gone, and was afraid he wouldn't return.

Five minutes later he knocked at the apartment door. He put down a brown paper bag from the convenience store in the basement and took out a quart of milk. I was as ashamed as I was grateful.

Our father was in Brazil, had been learning some Portuguese, and still seemed very pleased with his job. But before he left, he let me know, in an offhand way, that he might move on to something new. "How would you like to live in New York? It looks like a job offer might come through. Maybe you can come with me when I go up to find a place to live." But as usual there was no context, no explanation, and no time for questions. I didn't cause trouble. I didn't complain. I didn't make him feel like anything but an admirably good father.

It must have been that summer (after one of his trips to Texas, it seems likely now) that he surprised me by asking, "Do you think I should get married again?" He was leaning back in the oversized brown easy chair that went with the apartment, sipping a gin and tonic. I was no more prepared for that question than I'd been two years earlier when I was forced to say which parent I wanted to live with. This time I did not make the mistake of "choosing," but said only, "I think you should do whatever you need to do."

Nanny tried to fill in for our absent mother when and where she could. She often kept Sara and Ruthie overnight at her apartment across the river in Virginia, and sometimes we spent a whole weekend with her. She was a good cook, and, unlike our mother, enjoyed having someone to cook for. "Come and give me a kiss," was always the first thing she said when she came to our apartment, or we arrived at hers, and Sara and Ruthie were always ready to climb onto her lap. With me, though, she seemed uncertain whether she was supposed to take care of me, or vice versa. She might ask, "How do you think they're doing? They seem all right, don't they?" and I always said what I sensed she needed to hear—they were doing very well, we all were, and I could manage just fine.

I was grateful for her. Hers is the recipe I still use for spaghetti sauce, and if she were still alive she'd be pleased to know that. She took me to an Arlington fabric store for a pattern and two yards of butter-yellow linen, and let me use her sewing machine to make a summer jumper. "Oh, that's nice. It's wonderful how competent you are. I'm so glad your father doesn't have to worry about you, at least."

I'm not sure when I first heard my father say something similar—"At least you don't cause trouble"—and maybe he didn't say it often, but it was what I understood to be my role in the family now. Nanny didn't ask how I was doing in school; she had no idea how much of the time I wasn't going to school at all, and didn't know how few clothes I had, either. She worked full time as the bookkeeper for a women's club on Embassy Row, and she'd recently started a part-time business, making draperies for some of her club ladies. She had already taken a day off in June when my sisters and I needed checkups and shots and the forms we were going to need for new schools in the fall.

Sara hadn't seemed sick, but the doctor said she had to have her tonsils out. Summer was the only time for that, between the end of the school year and our next move. Sara would have to be at the hospital overnight, though, and Nanny couldn't take any more time off. "You can spend the night with her before the operation, can't you? And then I'll be able to come get you both the next evening. They say somebody has to stay with her."

I had agreed, of course, but didn't have any idea what I'd have to do. Nanny was doing her best to help my father pretend things were under control, and I was supposed to do the same for her.

Sara was very quiet when we arrived at Doctor's Hospital, and held tight to my hand, through the stop for paperwork at the admissions desk, the elevator to the pediatric floor, a nurses' station, and finally a tiny room smelling of rubbing alcohol and disinfectant and clean linen. Nanny and I got her into the hospital gown and into the narrow bed. "Now, you'll be just fine." Nanny hugged Sara and gave her another kiss. "Go to sleep and you'll forget being hungry, and by this time tomorrow you'll be having all the ice cream you want! Won't that be nice?"

I would spend the night sleeping, or at least resting, on a green vinyl recliner in the corner of the room.

"I have to go now, but Irene will be right here."

Sara's operation would be in the morning and Nanny could pick us up before suppertime the next day. She pulled out her wallet, counted a few bills and pressed them into my hand, frowning. "There's a cafeteria, I'm sure. You can get some breakfast tomorrow once they've taken her to surgery. Will that be okay?" It has to be okay. I have to make it be okay.

The next morning the window was gray, then gradually a bit lighter, and when I leaned closer I could see a wedge of blue sky high above, between this wing of the hospital and a neighboring high-rise. *It's going to be a nice day*, I thought. *Too bad Sara won't be seeing it.* The backs of my legs stuck to the vinyl, and I had a crick in my neck and a sour taste in my mouth. I hadn't thought of bringing a toothbrush. The yellow linen jumper that worked as a sundress now that the weather was getting hotter looked like it had been slept in, which of course it had. I slipped my dirty feet into brown leather sandals.

Sara wasn't quite awake, and after the nurse came in and put a needle in her arm (she only whimpered a little), she was asleep again and I dozed a bit more until the nurse and an orderly come in to take her away. The nurse said that it would be quite a while before Sara came back up to her room.

I was probably supposed to wait. Did I know that for sure? I felt disconnected from everything and everybody, and I needed to get somewhere and to someone so that I would stop feeling that I didn't exist.

I don't remember a cafeteria or any breakfast, only Sara being wheeled away. Then I was leaving the hospital and walking fast through the downtown streets until I found a pay phone. I had Lucky's number memorized, and he answered. His mother was at work, and somehow we decided this was the day I had to go to see the National Cathedral. He told me what bus to catch and promised to meet me at the Woodley Road stop. "You'll see the cathedral from blocks away. Just pull the cord as the bus starts to pass it, and the driver will let you off at the right place."

THE GOOD POETIC MOTHER

The D.C. Transit bus showed up before I had a chance to start worrying I'd gotten something wrong about the directions. As it wheezed its way up Wisconsin Avenue I caught sight of the pale stone tower, sailing above the trees like a ship, and pulled the cord. Then the bus was at the curb and there was Lucky, grinning. As we walked down Wisconsin Avenue we talked about where Patti had gone, about the fact that I was moving soon, and about him going to Connecticut to join the Submarine Corps. He seemed to be both excited and nervous about that. I wished he'd hold my hand, but he wasn't, as much as I wished it, really my boyfriend.

"They started building this thing fifty years ago, and they'll be working on it for another fifty." He pointed out the South Transept, with a massive limestone tower looming above. "When it's finished, there will be two more towers at the other end." I tried to imagine the completed building without the ugly tangle of scaffolding, and almost succeeded.

"Don't turn around yet." Lucky pushed his brown hair off his forehead, his voice intense with excitement. He had told me I couldn't leave D.C. without seeing the cathedral that had always been his favorite place in the city. Like me, he was born here, but unlike me, he had never left.

We had walked through the Bishop's Garden, a timeless walled sanctuary of huge boxwoods, rosemary, and lavender, with tea roses in a sunny formal bed in the center. Lucky led me through the smaller chapels, up and down narrow stone steps, and finally into the vast interior nave, where a kaleidoscope of color glowed on the stone floor before us. "You're going to see something amazing. Turn around and look up."

The massive rose window was far overhead. "You can't tell from here how big it is. But see the smaller circles around the edge? The eight separate ones? Each one of those has the figure of a saint. That's pretty cool, but get this—each one is life-sized!" I couldn't make out the saints, and it was impossible to gauge the size. What I could clearly see was how much in love Lucky was with this place. He'd known the cathedral and its grounds since elementary school, when his pure treble got him into the famous choir. The singing brought a scholarship, and those years were probably the happiest of his life. But when his voice changed he couldn't be a boy soprano any more, and didn't make the tenor section. That meant no more choir and no more music scholarship; he had been cast out of the most perfect place he'd ever known.

I didn't know if my throat ached because his story was so sad, or because I felt the same about Ann Arbor, longing to be back there, in what I still thought of as my real life. He could visit the cathedral, and maybe someday I'd see Ann Arbor again, but neither of us would ever really go home.

The time at the cathedral passed quickly and it was probably well past noon when Lucky reminded me of the little sister I'd put out of my mind while I was with him. "You need to get back to the hospital. You know you can't leave her there alone." I didn't want to go back, but was too ashamed to say so. I let Lucky walk me to the bus stop, where he waited until the bus came and we said our goodbyes. It was the last time I saw him.

Sara was already in her room when I arrived at the hospital. She was asleep, and I hoped everything was okay.

It wasn't. A nurse bustled in. "Are you her mother? Where have you been? Didn't they tell you somebody was supposed to stay with her today?" She was obviously surprised when I said I was Sara's sister, and within the hour I heard Nanny's heels, clicking fast on the linoleum. Then she was in the room, staring down at me in her slate-blue dress with rows of narrow tucks across the ample bodice. As always, she was perfectly dressed, managing to look elegant despite her large frame. Her lips were a thin line, blue eyes icy behind her rimless glasses.

"How could you do this to me? I can't believe you let me down like this. Can you imagine how I felt when that nurse called me at work to say nobody was with Sara? Terrible, just terrible." Nanny didn't want to hear that I'd only gone out for a while or that I'd thought I'd be back before Sara's surgery was over. I was in disgrace.

That's the only time I remember Nanny being angry at me. At the time, and for long after, I remembered this as my unforgiveable failure, an episode in which I had been the one abandoning a child. I've never been able to think about that day without being awash with shame and even, irrationally, re-experiencing the terror that my father might find out what I'd done. Mostly I remembered the unbearable fact of Nanny's anger—not with her son, or her former daughter-in-law or even Patti—but with me.

I got a letter from my mother that summer. Eight pages in blue, then red ballpoint, on thin letter paper torn from a pad, with no return address or date, only "Saturday." She began, "By the time you get this, no doubt Sara's operation will be all over. It is certainly good of you to agree to spend the night in the hospital with her. Knowing that you will be with her calms my fears." She didn't want to talk to Sara on the phone if she couldn't control her own anxiety; thought perhaps she'd send a letter, or call later, or something. The remaining pages were about her conflicted feelings about her own mother, her poetry, and musings about the meaning of life. She made more than one reference to the poet she was spending time with, mentioning "Charles" and "C" and later "Hank."

Almost as an afterthought, she mentioned Patti, who, I learned now for the first time, was living with Grandma Dean that summer. "In Mother's house I seem to put on a whole different character, I do not know what it is. Anyway I do know it's better for me to be out of it. After Patti goes home I will just cut off communication with Mother entirely until, anyway, such time as I know better what makes me tick where she is concerned."

What did she mean by *after Patti goes home*? Patti wasn't coming back to this home, that much was clear to me.

Mama enclosed one of her own poems. Her new poet friend "liked this one, which I recited to him in a flush of self-esteem in between some poems of his that he was reading to me."

> *NURSERY, '63*
> *There is a plant called hearts-ease...*
> *...in your garden, children.*
> *Learn to be good gardeners*
> *while we prepare for your funeral.*
> *There are no bleeding hearts in real life.*

That letter was the first time I heard of Henry Charles Bukowski ("Hank," to his friends). By the time my mother was pregnant with his child, I would be well down the path of trying not to care about her, concentrating on being as different from her as possible. That meant, of course, that I did my best not to learn anything at all about the Great Poet.

DON'T THINK (NEW YORK, 1963)

"Irene, can you stay after for a minute?" The bell shrilled and the hallway outside my tenth-grade English class echoed with raised voices as upperclassmen headed for the cafeteria. Mr. Savarino was gathering up a pile of book reports, stuffing them into a battered leather satchel with his gradebook. What could he want? I'd handed in my report; didn't think I'd missed any assignments. I liked his class, and I thought maybe he even liked me. I stood awkwardly in front of his desk, shifting from foot to foot.

There was one book left on the oak desk, and he picked it up. "You're doing very well in here." I let out my breath. "You moved here from Washington, is that right?" I nodded, hoping he wouldn't ask me about my old school. "Your father was in the government?" This seemed to be a good thing. My stomach rumbled—I wasn't so nervous now, got a whiff from the lunchroom of what might be sloppy joes, and wondered if I was going to get there in time to eat.

"I think you can read at a more advanced level." I glanced at the hardbound book in Mr. Savarino's hand. The dustjacket showed a nude woman, gripped from behind by a shadowy monster, and I quickly shifted my eyes back to the teacher. "I'm going to suggest some more challenging reading for you."

He handed me the book—William Faulkner, a name I recognized but knew nothing about. "Read the first few chapters, then come talk to me about it."

So Mr. Savarino thought I was smart. That, even more than his warm smile, made me feel like a completely different person—not a lost kid who didn't know her way around or what to wear, who didn't even have a mother, but someone else. I'd have friends, my teachers would like me, and my father would have to like me too. At four o'clock, I came home almost skipping—excited and cheerful and hopeful, looking forward to sharing my good news. I couldn't wait to—

It wasn't until I closed the back door behind me that I realized I'd been getting ready to tell Mama all about it, that I'd been having a conversation with her in my head, asking her about *The Sound and the Fury* and another book I remembered her reading that I thought was also by this Faulkner person. I hadn't spoken to her in more than a year, and my life was starting to become more manageable as I thought about her less, but the daydream I'd been lost in all the way home brought her back. I'd forgotten she was gone, and when I remembered the truth, it was like putting my foot through a hole in the floor. That brief spell of happy optimism evaporated and I felt not only the loss of her, but the bleakness of my life and how unworthy I must be.

Mr. Savarino is just pretending to like me, or if he does like me that's because he doesn't really know me yet. I'll never be able to read that book. I'll probably fail his class and he'll know what I'm really like.

THE GOOD POETIC MOTHER

We were living in Westchester County that fall, because our father was now the director of the consumer's magazine that our parents used to subscribe to. The salary was a lot more than his government job, and every few months they gave him a new car to drive when they finished testing a particular model. He talked about the "perks" of his position, and exactly how much he was paid, and I nodded and acted impressed. I was good at that.

And miraculously, even after everything that had happened in D.C., I was in tenth grade. Last spring, when Nanny took me to get my records from Jefferson Junior High, I thought I was going to throw up when the woman behind the counter told us I hadn't passed ninth grade. In the half year since we left Ann Arbor to crowd into our father's apartment, there had been too many days when I hadn't gone to school, but somehow I'd hoped there was still a chance—a kind of magical thinking that I should have outgrown—that as I finally got away from that school I'd also get out of ninth grade.

My father took me over to Hastings-on-Hudson High School at the end of August, and talked to the guidance counselor while I waited in the hall. After what seemed like a very long time, she came out, smiled, and beckoned for me to join them. Then she said, not to me but to my father, words that I have never forgotten: "Well, why don't we try her in tenth grade, and see how she gets on?" I didn't hear anything after that.

I had my own room now. Not shared with Sara and Ruthie (like in the apartment in Washington) or in the basement (like in the Ann Arbor house), and because we were renting furniture along with the house, there was a real bed with legs and a headboard, and a dresser and even a chair and a desk. The glazed chintz curtains—white roses and green leaves on a pink background—matched the bed's dust ruffle. I thought it was kind of conventional but I was far from caring whether or not any of this was my style.

I can see now that I didn't have any "style" of my own. The dislocations and neglect of the past two years, and maybe my mother's erratic attention even before that, had made me almost pathologically adaptable. If this room had old-fashioned curtains and ruffles, and my father had chosen this house, then that was what I liked, too. I was forgetting butterfly chairs and Danish modern coffee tables.

My own room meant I could close the door, play my guitar and sing, with no one to hear me. I was working my way through *The Young Folk Songbook*, learning the chords to all of Joan Baez' songs and a few by Bob Dylan and Peggy Seeger. I knew I had a nice voice, especially if no one was comparing me to Patti, and I imagined singing for Lucky or Mr. Berg—the music teacher I'd last seen more than a year ago.

But my own room was also where I sometimes woke up hours before the alarm, watching the sheer curtains inexorably lighten, turning over in my mind plausible excuses to stay home from school, just for a day. There was no reason to hate school, and I didn't, and I knew by now that falling behind, not turning in work, and missing school would mean disaster. But sometimes the chintz quilt seemed to be made of lead.

Our father was going to get married again. She lived in Texas and they'd met when he was visiting the Peace Corps' language school in Austin. He said she was in graduate school, mentioned "Phi Beta Kappa" more than once, and if I hadn't known what that meant before, I did now. He had a picture of her, and when I asked how old she was (I meant in the picture) he said tersely, "Twenty-six." I could tell he didn't want me to say anything about that, and I didn't care how old she was, anyway. It was the little kids who needed her; I'd be gone in three more years and nobody had to know she wasn't actually old enough to be my mother.

We hadn't met her, and I understood that it was too far for her to come here during their engagement, and certainly too expensive for all of us to go to Texas for the wedding. I was glad that there was going to be someone to take care of my sisters and that I wouldn't have to come straight home after school every day. Now that I had a friend I wanted to be able to go across the street to Cecilia's house sometimes. I liked her mother and she liked me and maybe (I didn't like to admit this) that mattered more to me than my friendship with Cecilia.

The high school and the town seemed more like Ann Arbor than like D.C., and even though I was lost at first, and always worried about being late to class, it was getting easier. Most of the time I felt better once I got to school, and even when I was by myself in the afternoon, if I forced myself to work on some assignment I could hold off the dark mood for a while. I thought of asking for a sewing machine, and imagined clothes I might make that would help me fit in. I had tried out for the choir, and if I could get permission to stay after school for practice, maybe I'd stop being overcome so often by gloom and inertia.

That was the day I finally figured out what to do. It was remembering the people who were gone, thinking about the life I had *before,* that brought on the darkness, and suddenly the solution was clear. I was just not going to think about anybody or anything that I missed, anything that might make me sad. I wasn't going to think about Mama or imagine telling her I was reading Faulkner. I wouldn't wonder about Patti and whether she might teach me the harmony to "Golden Vanity," or remember Nanny and imagine what school clothes she might help me sew, or reminisce about my friend Lucky and the way he used to whistle all the way down Fourth Street. I wouldn't remind myself about the National Gallery and walking through the echoing rotunda, and definitely not think about the Japanese cherry trees in front of the church on Washtenaw Avenue in Ann Arbor, or the broad steps in front of the school on East University, or our house on Morningside Drive, or my oldest friend Sally or my boyfriend Jim. These were all things I couldn't afford to think of any longer—whatever comfort it might be to see them in my mind was more than outweighed by the pain and paralysis that came over me when I realized how much was gone.

So I simply stopped. *Just don't think about it*, I said to myself. *Switch to something else, something about now.* I tried it out, and found that I could actually shut down a memory, just as it started to take shape, and that it wasn't even that hard. *What's for dinner …Nanny's recipe for meatloaf* …No. Stop. Later. Look at my desk, look out the window, across the street to the Cecilia's house. Think about going for a walk with her, here in the pretty village of Hastings. *What's that song Patti used to* …I wouldn't sing songs she used to sing. I had plenty of others in the songbook. I didn't need to know what Mama might think of *The Sound and the Fury*, and if I could get a sewing machine I could make clothes without Nanny's help. I didn't feel like crying anymore. I felt kind of disconnected from everything, even from myself, but I didn't feel bad.

I worried some, even at fifteen, about the long-term effectiveness of this surprisingly-easy deliberate forgetting. It was my mother, I think, whose doubt I imagined, which means I knew that despite her instability she believed in honesty, in not fooling oneself. But she was gone, and I had to find a way to keep going. What I couldn't have understood, and wouldn't fully recognize until after she died, is that I was doing exactly what she herself had done. Once she'd given up trying to take care of her daughters, and after the papers she had signed turned out to give us all to our father, she began to consider that part of her life as irretrievable, irrevocably in the past. She couldn't think about what she'd left behind and face going on with her life.

SICK DAY (NEW YORK, 1964)

It was just after two in the morning, and Sara was standing at my bedroom door sobbing. I'd been dreaming about hearing a child crying and trying to find her, and now there she was, saying she was sick and that Ruthie was awake and didn't feel well either. I turned on the light and went to their room and Ruthie was holding her stomach and whimpering. Thank goodness Sara got herself to the bathroom in time, I thought. I ran down to the kitchen and came back with two big mixing bowls and put one by each bed. Sara said she felt better, but about twenty minutes later Ruthie threw up, and then Sara did again, and I was feeling kind of queasy myself even though I was pretty sure it was just because of the smell. I flushed the throw-up down the toilet and rinsed out the bowls in the bathtub and brought them back and got Ruthie a clean nightgown since she hadn't gotten it all in the bowl. I was upset and kind of mad at them and a little rough getting Ruthie changed. But I brought in the wicker chair from my room and sat with them until they went back to sleep, then left both their door and mine open and went back to my own room. I was just starting to worry about the next day but hoped that by morning they'd be better and could go to school, and then I could, too.

My father and stepmother had left so quickly that I still wasn't sure what the trip was about or how long they would be gone or why they both had to go. We'd met our stepmother back in February, after the wedding in Texas that my sisters and I had not attended. She was very young, quite pretty, and, I thought, not very happy to be taking care of someone else's three girls. It was November now, and I was keeping my head down, trying not to think about her too much.

Whatever the reason for their trip to Washington, I knew what my responsibilities were. I was to take care of Sara and Ruthie, make sure they got up on time and dressed for school and had breakfast and didn't miss the bus; take one of the prepared meals out of the freezer and leave it to defrost during the day; make sure to be home from school by the time the girls arrived; fix them a snack and make sure Sara did her homework and do my own; heat up dinner; make them get to bed on time.

The trip would be only for a few days, I thought. Certainly my father and stepmother would be back sometime that weekend. It meant I couldn't get to school early for choir practice on Thursday morning, and we'd been working hard on the Vivaldi "Gloria." Still, I'd memorized the second soprano part and the music director liked me and I didn't think he'd give me a demerit. I would have to come directly home at three, and couldn't linger with the other juniors and seniors on the back steps. But after being responsible for my younger sisters so much back in D.C., and for the first six months after we moved here to Hastings, being in charge for a few days wasn't going to be a problem. A small part of me felt important and an even smaller part hoped, as always, that maybe this would be the thing my father would notice, and appreciate, and approve of.

We'd had to move out of the furnished brick house across the street from Cecilia's when the owners came back from overseas. Now we were a mile south, just above the Hudson, in a white clapboard Dutch colonial that the rental agent said used to be a cider mill. (There was supposed to be a bricked-up tunnel in the basement where the cider barrels had been rolled down to the river.) I thought my stepmother would have liked something newer, but the age and history of the place appealed to me deeply. It was the first time I'd lived in a house with a fireplace or a separate dining room, and in a familiar way I began to believe in some miraculous familial transformation.

I had claimed a tiny unfurnished attic room, up a flight of stairs from my bedroom, where I sat on the floor with an old couch cushion and a quilt, reading and sometimes looking out through the wavy panes of the single window. Gazing across the rooftops and trees to the Palisades on the far side of the Hudson River gave me a romantic, dreamy feeling, as if I were actually living the life I'd always wished was mine. In a house so classic and traditional, the people living in it would surely be loving and kind and stable, and I'd have a secure home. In some mysterious way it would make me safe, forever. I'd given up thinking about the past, and had gotten even better at escaping into an imagined future.

Cecilia and I were still best friends. Well, to be honest, I was her best friend, but now that she wasn't my *only* friend I wasn't sure I felt the same about her. She was two years younger and that made more of a difference now. It was too bad we didn't live on the same street anymore, but it was only a twenty-minute walk to her house. We didn't see each other at school because the freshmen and the juniors didn't hang out together and it would have been weird if I talked to her there.

When I was with Cecilia I was still a kid—we talked and giggled and had adventures and spoke French to each other when we got to take the train into the city, walking around Greenwich Village (while her mother thought we were at Bloomingdale's and the Metropolitan Museum). But when I was with friends my own age I felt more like the sixteen-year-old I was. After the first time I sort of accidentally didn't see Cecilia looking for me after school, she went home alone and neither of us said anything about it. I was sometimes bored with her, but at the same time not in a big hurry to act older. There had been more than enough of that in the year we lived with my mother.

On Thursday I was home by three-thirty and Sara and Ruthie came from the bus stop at a quarter of four. I fixed cinnamon toast for all of us, with tea for myself and milk for them, and made Sara show me the worksheet she had to do for Friday. She didn't need any help with her fourth-grade work and Ruthie, in first grade, didn't get homework yet. She could read pretty well now and I gave her a couple of picture books and she bent over them with her cute little glasses and serious face and we had our own study hall. I did some trigonometry and went over a review sheet for civics but I'd already finished reading my English assignment and by dinner time we were all done.

The beef stew had been defrosting in the sink all day, and I began to heat it up. When Sara said she didn't like stew and asked if there was anything else to eat I got very stern with her. "No, I said there's stew. You can have that or you can skip dinner." I don't know if she noticed how much I sounded like our mother (who could never abide complaints about the food she served), but she stopped arguing and Ruthie didn't start.

SICK DAY (NEW YORK, 1964)

Sometimes I thought they didn't know how lucky they were. When Patti and I were their ages we were doing laundry and cooking dinner most of the time—and taking care of the two of them, for that matter. At least now they had a mother who got up in the morning and made sure there was food to eat, and they weren't always late for school.

My stepmother called at seven. They were coming back on Saturday, or Sunday at the latest, and she would telephone again the next evening. I recited everything I'd done, but she didn't say anything except to remind me to put all the mail on the kitchen table and to save the *New York Times* for my father.

A while later Cecilia called, too. I hadn't seen her at school, and of course couldn't stop at her house afterwards. She'd been home sick, couldn't keep anything down. Her mother was letting her try some crackers, but she'd probably have to stay home one more day. Maybe we would get together on the weekend if she was better and my parents were back.

By eight it was time for bed. I thought about giving the girls baths but figured no one would know if I skipped them, and they didn't care anyway. Now that the day was almost over I wasn't annoyed with them and felt like being nicer, and so I offered to read to them. Somehow I still had my copy of *Little House on the Prairie*. After two chapters, they begged for more but I was bored. "That's enough. I'm turning off the light and I don't want to hear anything out of you until morning."

Downstairs, I washed the dishes and dried them and put them away and swept the kitchen floor. I knew now that it wasn't good enough to just have the counters clear and the dishes washed and the sink empty. When our stepmother first came, I'd hoped she'd see how helpful I could be, and what a good job I did around the house. Maybe I'd imagined we'd be allies, or even friends, but she had not been pleased the first time I cleaned up after dinner. I don't remember how long I wondered what her thin-lipped silence was about, or when she finally said something about being shocked that I didn't even know that the kitchen floor was supposed to be swept after dinner every single day.

Sometime after the move to the cider mill house, six-year-old Ruthie had gotten in trouble for telling one of the neighbors too much about the family. Apparently she'd confided that she had another big sister, and that this sister had a baby of her own, which meant that little Ruthie was an aunt. That had happened in February, just a week after our father and stepmother got married. Seven months after that, our mother had given birth to Bukowski's daughter, and I guess Ruthie told this neighbor about her real mother who lived in California, and about a new baby sister none of us had ever seen. The sisters part might have been okay, but the parts about the baby and the real mother and the other baby definitely weren't. Our stepmother (who had insisted, with our father's support, that Sara and Ruthie begin calling her Mommy at the very beginning), now said Ruthie was a stupid little blabbermouth, as if she should have known without being told that it was forbidden to talk about certain things. I knew that was unfair, and I felt bad for Ruthie, but I didn't stick up for her. I didn't want anyone knowing things like that about us either—that Patti had run away and gotten pregnant or that our mother was on welfare out in California, living with some poet she wasn't married to.

Somebody always being in trouble at home didn't fit with the life I wished we had, either; so Ruthie needed to get better at not making our stepmother mad. I was still trying to be cooperative and follow the rules so that Ruthie and Sara could have a chance to have a mother again, and didn't have much patience for any of their complaints.

SICK DAY (NEW YORK, 1964)

My plan still wasn't working out very well. Somebody had always done something wrong, and should have known what it was, and it seemed like our stepmother was always just about out of patience.

I decided to go to bed early myself, propped up on the pillows for a while reading more of the Laura Ingalls Wilder book even though I'd outgrown it, and then I turned out my light too.

Before my alarm went off, I heard Ruthie in the bathroom. Now she had diarrhea and her panties were messed and she was weeping like somebody had died. She couldn't stop sobbing and I felt bad about not being nicer to her last night. I cleaned her up and got fresh underwear and got her back to bed and told her getting sick wasn't her fault. I knew that she hated more than anything to make a mistake, and I thought it was partly because our stepmother pretty much treated her as if everything she did was wrong. I sometimes treated her that way, too.

Now I was awake and considering my options. I could tell that the girls weren't really better even though I tried to convince myself they were, but I told them they should get dressed "in case you're well enough to go to school." Sara did put on some clothes but said she couldn't eat breakfast, and Ruthie didn't even try and went back to sleep. It was starting to dawn on me that I probably couldn't expect them to go to school. But if they stayed home, then I'd have to stay home too, and that would be what had been called being *truant* back in D.C. Missing school had become one of my top things-not-to-do. Along with the don't-think-about-it rule (about Mama and Patti and Nanny and other people and places and things), making sure I didn't stay home, no matter how I felt, was the one way I could make sure that what happened in ninth grade never would again. As long as I didn't skip, and didn't fall behind, I wouldn't be in trouble; my teachers wouldn't be angry at me and other kids wouldn't make fun of me, and my parents wouldn't have another reason to hate me. But that meant I absolutely could not be absent without permission.

Nobody was there to give me that permission, and my parents wouldn't be calling until that night and I didn't have a phone number for them or know where they were staying in Washington and I wasn't supposed to make a long-distance call anyway. I got dressed, almost as if I thought something might happen by magic to solve this. It was seven-thirty, and if I were going to school I'd have to leave by eight. Could I call the high school office? Who would I talk to? How could I explain? Somehow I knew that I couldn't say my parents were away and my sisters were sick and I had to stay home with them. I didn't want to have to tell anyone that my father left town so suddenly and made our stepmother come too. (I think now that's how it must have been—I can imagine him saying, "And you're coming with me!" and my stepmother, like my mother before her, unable to argue.)

Maybe the girls could stay home without me? I'd been home sick and alone plenty of times when I was in elementary school. It hadn't been too bad, lying in Mama's bed, getting up to take my medicine when the timer went off. I listened to the radio and even though I sometimes feared she'd never come home, I grew out of that. Sara was old enough now to be in charge of Ruthie and she could make their lunch—I couldn't quite convince myself that plan would be okay. I might get in trouble if anybody found out I left them by themselves, even if I did it in order to get to school myself. And the girls might tell, even if I made them promise not to. And really, something about leaving them alone made *me* feel a bit sick.

Then I remembered that Cecilia might not be going to school. She was almost fourteen, old enough to babysit. Could she, would she, maybe …well, at least I could talk to her about it. The truth was that she liked me more than I liked her and when I was especially

SICK DAY (NEW YORK, 1964)

nice to her she'd do anything I wanted. So I dialed her number and although Mr. Marchetti sounded surprised to hear from me so early, he had Cecilia pick up the upstairs phone.

"I was calling to see if you're feeling better this morning," I began. "Are you going to school today?" Maybe it could sound like I just wanted to see her. She said she felt a lot better but still couldn't eat much and had to stay home another day. Perfect.

So I told her about Sara and Ruthie and how I was sure they were okay now but, like her, probably not quite well enough to go to school. "I already had to miss choir yesterday, and I need to get my assignments in because if they're late I'll lose points, and I think there's going to be a quiz in chemistry today too." I made up the story about a quiz but Cecilia was in different classes and couldn't know that. "I don't think they're really sick anymore but—" She didn't offer any ideas so I had to come out and ask her if maybe her parents would let her come over to my house for the day and just be there with my sisters. Sara and Ruthie could take care of themselves, so she wouldn't have to do anything, and that way I could go to school. "I'll come home right after school and so it won't be any later than three-thirty." I guess I was thinking none of them were really, *really* sick. Or something.

"Well, maybe, but I'll have to ask my dad. Hold on a minute." I heard her calling for her father, and crossed my fingers. But then it was Mr. Marchetti on the phone. "What's going on, Irene?" he asked. He didn't sound exactly mad but he wasn't as friendly as usual, not kidding me like he usually did, and I stammered out something about my sisters being sick and me not having permission to stay home and my parents being away "for the day" and Cecilia and me thinking maybe she could come over here since she's not going to school anyway and—

THE GOOD POETIC MOTHER

"And what, so they can sit around and watch each other puke?" he snorted. "What are you thinking? She can't come over there, she's not going anywhere. You're just going to have to stay home, I guess. Sorry she can't help you out."

He hung up. He had never been angry with me before, always said I was "a good kid," that I was very mature and responsible for my age, and I thought he liked me. Now he knew I was not a nice person at all, had been trying to take advantage of Cecilia, and wasn't a good friend to her. He would stop trying to see anything good in me, just like Nanny had seemed to when I left my little sister in the hospital last year. It didn't matter if it was fair or not.

I don't remember much more. I must have stayed home. My sisters got better, I didn't get sick myself, and the next day was Saturday. By Monday our parents were back and I must have gotten some sort of note to take to school. I don't remember what either of them said about what had happened, but I got a definite sense that it was a bad time for any new problems.

My father had lost his New York job, and the reason he and my stepmother went to D.C. in such a hurry had been to talk to some people about getting a new one. Things were even more silent and tense when they first returned, but after a few days and many phone calls, he became upbeat, saying that because Johnson was staying in the White House there were lots of great opportunities for him as the New Frontier became the Great Society. I knew I was supposed to know why this was such good news, but the only thing I really understood is that we were not going to be living in Hastings much longer.

He wasn't going back to the Peace Corps, where he'd been before we came to Westchester, but would help run something called the Job Corps, part of Johnson's War on Poverty. They'd rented a house in Maryland and said that the schools in Montgomery County were the best anywhere. I was supposed to appreciate the trouble they'd gone to, and of course I was glad we wouldn't be back in the city, but I wasn't sure I believed anything about the schools. Or maybe I didn't care. I just knew we were moving, that it was the middle of my junior year, that everything I'd figured out about how to fit in here was useless now, and that I was about to be the new kid one more time.

Cecilia's parents must have forgiven me for trying to get her to take care of my sick little sisters, because after the rest of my family left for Maryland I stayed with the Marchettis for the last weeks of the fall term. My parents made some kind of agreement with Cecilia's, and there was some money involved, and for a brief while I imagined that, if I could present it in just the right way, I might be able to stay in Hastings for the rest of my junior year. Then, maybe, I could go on living with them until I finished high school. After all, Cecilia's oldest brother was already gone, and her other brother would be going to college soon, so they'd have an extra room. I talked to Cecilia about it until it seemed like something we both wanted, and she agreed to bring it up with her folks. I planned to ask my stepmother about it in our next Sunday phone call.

By the time I knew that my parents weren't going to spend any more money for my room and board, Cecilia had told me it wasn't okay with her folks either. "They say it wouldn't work out," is all she would say, and I was too humiliated to ask for any details. It was starting to feel that getting away from her, from them, from Hastings was maybe a good idea after all.

MEET YOUR SISTER (WASHINGTON, 1965)

We'd been in Bethesda for about four months, in a nice-enough house in a nice-enough neighborhood, only a couple of blocks away from the elementary school where my sisters would be in first and fourth grades. I had to take the bus, but the high school was, as advertised, quite civilized, with challenging but kind teachers and no fighting in the hallways. I had joined the junior class midway through the year, but the girl who sat next to me in homeroom was friendly and I gradually began to find my way around the sprawling building.

And now our mother, whom I hadn't seen since our last day in Ann Arbor two-and-a-half years earlier, had decided to come for a visit. She took the bus from Los Angeles with the baby, and when I heard that plan I remembered the train trip she and I made over the same distance when I was small. She didn't like to fly, apparently; thought it too dangerous or maybe too bourgeois. And she never had any money.

Of course I'd known about my half-sister—I recalled a letter from my mother saying she was pregnant, but then got it confused with

MEET YOUR SISTER (WASHINGTON, 1965)

a poem she'd written about her "darling pregnant daughter." Patti's baby had been born a year ago, on Valentine's Day, perhaps just as my mother was realizing that she herself was expecting. But those babies were off-screen events, completely separate from my suburban East Coast life, and precisely the kind of things never spoken of by the people with whom I lived. I'd left Ann Arbor for Washington, relocated to New York, acquired a stepmother, come south again to a D.C. suburb, and gone from ninth to tenth and now to eleventh grade. I hadn't been thinking much about my older sister or my mother, and even less about a new half-sister.

We sat together at the yellow kitchen table. I was wearing a flowered skirt and blouse with a Peter Pan collar and tucked bodice that made it look, I hoped, like one of the Villager outfits that were popular here. My mother's loose gray jumper, over a black leotard and tights, contrasted with both my own blue-and-white print and the baby's pink terry pajamas.

Then the baby sneezed. Now, when we were growing up with our mother, there were always books, and she read to us a lot, and sometimes favorite lines became shared jokes. We'd all liked the scene in *Alice in Wonderland* involving a duchess and her baby and a crazy cook and too much pepper, and in our house when someone sneezed, instead of saying "bless you," one of us might recite the duchess's verse, which I did now: "Speak roughly to your little boy, and beat him when he sneezes. He only does it to annoy, because he knows it teases." It was the kind of not-too-sweet thing my mother liked, I remembered, but she was not amused. She was looking at the flushed and fretful baby on her lap.

THE GOOD POETIC MOTHER

"She might be coming down with a cold," my mother said, wiping Marina's little nose with a diaper. "The bus was crowded, and there were a lot of people coughing and sneezing. And of course it's so much colder here than in L.A."

The resentment I'd managed to suppress—during the two days she'd been here, during the thirty months since we last lived together—began rising to the surface. It was April, and winter was over. *It's not cold,* I thought. *It's beautiful here! It's springtime in Washington, and you used to say you loved it!* I remembered making the trip from Michigan to Washington with her, to visit Nanny in the 1950s, and later to see where we were going to live in the early 1960s. Michigan might still be gray, but by Pittsburgh we'd see forsythia, then redbud trees after Cumberland, and dogwoods by the time we drove into D.C. I'd noticed the progression of blooms then, and remembered later, because my mother drew our attention to those things, because I could see her pleasure in them, and because, of course, they were lovely. But now she thought Los Angeles was the only place worth living, and that was really something, wasn't it? She'd gone back to California like she always promised us we all would.

"I think maybe she's running a fever. Maybe we should give her a bath. Would you like to help me do that?"

I thought it would have been better not to have taken a baby on a bus for five days, and I didn't think she was going to like a bath if she was feverish. But my job was to agree and to help. Mama started to unbutton the little pajamas. "Wash out the sink, okay? So we can bathe her in there. And then find me a bath towel."

"Oh, the sink's clean," I said brightly. "It doesn't need to be scrubbed." Because for one thing my stepmother kept house quite thoroughly, and for another it was my job to wash the supper dishes, and dry them and put them away, and there was nothing in the sink.

MEET YOUR SISTER (WASHINGTON, 1965)

Unlike, I did not say, every sink in every kitchen in every house I'd ever lived in with my mother, where the dishes would pile up and stay that way until our father came home and started yelling about the "pigsty," and then it would be me and Patti who would have to clean up.

"It's clean already, but I'll bring you a towel." I stood up, smiling at the two of them. Then Mama got up too, and crossed to the sink, with the baby on her shoulder. We both looked at it. The stainless steel was spotless, but Mama ran two fingers around the inside of the bowl.

"No, I think it could be greasy. You can't tell looking at a sink like that if it's really clean or not. That's why I don't like a stainless steel sink. You need to wash it out with soap and hot water before we can give her a bath."

I opened the cupboard, found the Palmolive and a sponge, and slammed both on the counter.

"Is that sponge clean? Sometimes they get sour if you put them in a cupboard. It's really better to leave them out. People don't understand that. And actually it's better to use a dishcloth because you can wring it out and hang it up to dry."

I remembered the smelly rag in the kitchen sink on South Grove Road in Ypsilanti, not wanting to pick it up to wipe the table, and Mama rolling her eyes at me. I'm sure I hadn't appreciated being corrected by her even when she was still my mother, but now that she wasn't, I thought I should be excused forever from having to listen to her criticism.

I don't remember what we said to one another after that. I guess the baby got her bath, and probably fussed, and Mama took her off to the spare room and I wiped down the counters and went to bed myself. And thought I'd be happy if I never saw either of them again.

KEEPSAKES (WASHINGTON, 1965)

The little bear stands solidly on all fours in the palm of my hand, head and neck outstretched, a fat fish in its mouth. The unglazed black pottery is burnished to a dull gleam, and a faint crooked line shows where the right ear was once broken off and repaired. Something is written in pencil on the bear's belly—a few letters are recognizable, but I have never been able to make out the artist's name. The most striking thing about the bear is that I still have it.

My mother sent it to me sometime in the late 1980s. She'd gone to New Mexico, perhaps to visit my youngest sister at an ashram, and bought this Zuni fetish from a woman she met there. "I don't know if this is at all the kind of thing you like," she wrote in spidery ballpoint, "but it made me think of you. The bear with a fish is supposed to be a spirit guide. The people here say he will bring you what you need."

The bear was not the only thing she'd sent since leaving for Los Angeles in 1963, but it was one of the few gifts from her that I had managed to keep track of. Many things had been lost when our parents split up—my silver baby cup, my older sister's complete set of

Nancy Drew, almost all the family photographs—and after she left, the mementos I still had of my mother seemed to be filled with what Elizabeth Bishop called "the intent to be lost."

The first things to go were my mother's letters, along with the slippery onionskin carbon copies of poems she always enclosed. I didn't understand the poems, couldn't follow her radical ideas, and didn't want to hear about her poet friends and poet lover. I saw her give up Frances Dean Smith to be S. S. Veri, then Frances Dean Bukowski, and later on francEyE. She still signed her letters *Mama*, but I only sometimes thought of her that way.

I was fifteen, and she'd been gone less than a year, when I received not one but two copies of *It Catches My Heart in Its Hands*. Bukowski's breakout book was an art object as much as a collection of poems, letterpress on heavy deckled-edged pages in saturated shades of gold and blue and red. Both copies were signed by the author. The first was inscribed "To Irene Smith—of the good poetic mother. / Yrs. Charles Bukowski 8-3-63." A second volume (I have never known why I got two, just weeks apart) included a handwritten note from the publisher, saying the book was a gift from my mother. "Take good care of this—it is already a collectors' item, though just published." I was not inclined to take care of it. The physical beauty of the book seemed ruined by the skeleton on the cover, the photo of the rough-faced poet, and most of all by the poems—about whores and beer and vomit and a life that sounded even worse than what I'd already lived.

For my seventeenth birthday, my mother ordered for me a lithograph titled *Children and Doves*, by a New York artist transplanted to New Mexico, whose husband (a psychiatrist and a poet), was a Bukowski fan. The psychiatrist had sent a copy of his wife's prize-winning picture "to Hank, in response to his poems," my mother wrote;

THE GOOD POETIC MOTHER

she herself never tired of looking at the print, and was sure that I'd want to hang my copy where I could see it all the time.

She had rescued Hank's copy from being scotch-taped to a wall, and had pinned it to a piece of fabric which was now thumbtacked to their bedroom door. I, however, should have my copy matted and framed as soon as possible. She didn't actually know the artist, but the artist's husband (the psychiatrist-poet-Bukowski-fan) had written, at the time of Marina's birth, a poem "to be read aloud to her on her fifth birthday." Instead of waiting, Mama sang the poem to the baby already. It was their favorite song, she told me.

After telling me about the image and the artist and how I should be sure to take proper care of this latest gift, she revealed that she knew I had two copies of Bukowski's book. A friend of hers, she wrote, "is looking for a copy of *It Catches My Heart In Its Hands*, and may write to you to see if he can purchase one of yours. Don't hesitate to ask for enough ($7.50) to buy for yourself a copy of Hank's new book *Crucifix in a Deathhand*."

I put the letter down at that point. I didn't want any more poems, and didn't know where Bukowski's very special famous books were, even if I had wanted to sell one of them.

Then the picture arrived, direct from the artist's studio, rolled into a sturdy cardboard mailing tube. Children's faces, outstretched hands, doves flying. If I had been younger, and if my mother had still been "Mama," I would have agreed to like it.

The artist wrote to my mother as she was preparing to mail the print, and my mother forwarded that missive to me. I noted that it had been addressed to "Frances Bukowski," and remembered that Mama had said something about Bukowski letting her use his name. I wondered why, as much as she'd wanted to get out of a marriage, and as unconventional as she tried to be, she was pretending to be married.

KEEPSAKES (WASHINGTON, 1965)

"I must tell you," the artist had written to my mother, "that this is not just another sale to me." No, it was special and significant to her that someone in another state "would love your child enough to want to give her what touches you in a tender, loving way, and that you would babysit so many hours to do this, and that my work is what you want." Mama's letter hadn't said anything about babysitting, and this detail made me uneasy.

The artist went on to say how important it was to her to spend my mother's twenty dollars in a meaningful way, and how she had just bought two weavings from a poor, almost-forty and almost-divorced woman she'd happened to meet in Santa Fe, who was trying to do art but lacked confidence, poor thing.

Twenty dollars. I couldn't avoid the calculation: if Mama got fifty cents an hour for babysitting (as I did) then it would have taken forty hours to scrape together enough to buy the picture for me.

The newly-discovered weaver had "just completed her first two tapestries," both intended for children, and here the artist mentioned her own two sons. One of the weavings "is of a lion smelling a flower, and the other is of mice dancing under a tree. I am enchanted! Charles Bukowski, himself, wrote in a poem once something like this— 'Both the lion and the mouse know we are dead.' Could it be better? Your gift to your daughter becomes these to my sons. And, perhaps all of us have helped in the birth of a really fine artist."

I sensed that my mother and this other woman wanted me to recognize the value of the joint bequest, love it enough to be worthy of its beauty and multiple meanings, appreciate the privilege of being included in their circle of mutual admiration, and agree that it had been wonderful of my mother to babysit to make money to buy this amazing picture for me. They wouldn't want to know how many unpaid hours I had spent babysitting for my mother's children. I rolled up the lithograph, put it back in the mailing tube and leaned it against the wall of my closet.

All that was in July. In November, my mother wrote once more, mentioning the artist and her psychiatrist-Bukowski-fan husband. Bukowski had met the creator of the *Children and Doves* lithograph, and had described her in a poem as "run through with three simple things: drink, despair, loneliness—and two more: youth and beauty."

The artist had just been divorced by the psychiatrist, my mother wrote, "so he could marry somebody else's wife. I guess if she gets through the horrible first months, she may find her dove after all; her art is so great I can't believe she will let it go."

My mother and Bukowski separated soon after this communication, and the next letter I received from my mother was from a new address.

The unframed print stayed in the closet of my basement bedroom for more than a year, but before I left for college, I tried to give it (and myself, and maybe my mother) another chance. The mailing tube had softened where it made contact with the floor, breaking down like the disintegrating attachment between us. The print stuck to the cardboard, and although I tried to ease it gently out, there was a tear on one edge. Not too big, I noted, maybe some tape on the back would fix that. But when I unrolled the lithograph I saw that the bottom third of the print was damp and discolored, the smooth ivory paper stained brown with gray spots speckling the entire image. The picture was ruined, Mama's hours of babysitting counted for nothing, and I had thrown away what might be the last good thing I got from my mother. She had been thinking of me, was trying to make a connection and acknowledge that we were mother and daughter, but my sadness and hurt had hardened into bitterness, and I had to reject her gift along with the unwelcome accounts of her new friends and family.

In my twenties and thirties, I made more of an effort not to misplace the occasional poetry journal or chapbook she sent. I read each of her poems at least once, but the oddly-sized volumes slipped behind what I thought of as my real books. At least I didn't hate her anymore.

I have kept the little bear for three decades now. He sat on my desk through graduate school, came in my pocket to licensing exams, and for years occupied the top shelf of a cherry bookcase in my office.

"The people here tell me it's good luck," my mother had written. I don't know if I believe in luck, or if the bear with its fish brought me what I need. I thought I was past needing anything from her. Still, the people may have been right, because the bear is still here.

And so am I.

MANIFESTO (WASHINGTON, 1965)

The day's mail was still on the floor, and a fat envelope was stuck under the bottom of the foyer door when I came home from school. Postmarked "Los Angeles September 23, 1965," it was addressed to me from 5124 DeLongpre Avenue. That's where my mother lived with the Great Poet and their baby in a duplex bungalow I had never seen. It would, in 2013, be designated a Los Angeles Cultural Landmark, renamed "Bukowski Court," but my mother would remain there only two more months after she wrote this letter.

Feeling how thick the envelope was, I assumed it contained poems—my mother's, certainly; perhaps some by Bukowski or one of her other friends. The envelope was not quite large enough for the fat sheaf of pages inside and the flap was fastened crookedly with masking tape. I took it to my bedroom, put my books on the bed, and opened the envelope. I was relieved that there didn't seem to be any poems enclosed, but the twenty-two sheets of notebook paper, covered in an uneven scrawl, made me uneasy.

MANIFESTO (WASHINGTON, 1965)

She began her letter with a reference to her youngest daughter, the baby I had met six months earlier. "I don't seem to get any clear time to write anymore," she wrote. "Either I am sleeping more or Marina's sleeping less. I'm not sure which, but she seems to be always awake when I am now." After this mild complaint about the one-year-old, she turned to what seemed to be an invitation. She'd like to see me, to have me come to California for a visit. I was surprised and at first intrigued.

"I've had it in mind for some time to try and start saving some money so that, if you would like to and could, I could pay half your fare to come out here and visit me this year." She had opened a savings account, saved thirty-five dollars already, and hoped my father and stepmother would allow me to visit and perhaps share the cost. She mentioned college, and I was relieved that at least one of my parents was aware of this looming transition. "You probably know that people do come out here from all over because the universities are less expensive than elsewhere and have overall pretty high standards. An energetic young person can often become self-supporting fairly soon and still get a degree. It seems you ought to have a chance to look the situation over if you want to." Well, that was a novel thought. Some of my classmates had visited colleges over the summer, although that wasn't something my father and stepmother seemed to think necessary.

She mentioned my other little sisters, now ten and seven. Ruthie (she'd been five when our mother left) had recently written to her mama, asking her if she might come East again, maybe for Christmas. Our mother explained, as if simply reporting the weather, that she did "not want to do that—chiefly because neither Marina nor I really have any winter clothes." She made a vague attempt to consider the younger girls and what they might need or want, and "if it would be

-149-

possible for Sara to come out next year, Ruthie the year after that… or perhaps S & R are too young to travel so far alone."

Too young to travel so far alone. Did I remember then, reading this letter in 1965 (perhaps with the sharp resentment I feel even now), the Greyhound bus when I was thirteen or fourteen, and Sara and Ruthie something like six and four, and not ever being able to work out later whether we had been going from Ann Arbor to D.C., or in the other direction? Or why the three of us were traveling on our own? Did my mother remember that?

"I really would like to have a visit with you alone… if your father is not opposed." When had she started speaking of him in that formal way? And the harder question is why, really, did she want me to come to California? My clearest memory of her visit in the spring was of helping her take care of the baby. Was that what she had in mind now, to have a big girl to help her with the little one? Maybe it would give her more time to write?

Then came the most upsetting part of the letter. She believed she knew something of my life, and wanted to set me straight on a few things. Even if "it may be none of my business," she had taken as truth something Patti had told her, "that there was a big family confabulation over you and a boyfriend of yours who is a close friend of Rick's—Patti said that she thought your stepmother changed her attitude to one more favorable toward the boy when she found out that his father was a very rich man."

There had been no such family event, and I had no boyfriend at this point in my life, rich or otherwise. I barely knew my sister's husband, and had never met any friend of his. But Mama clearly believed Patti's story, and, be it her business or not, had a few things to say. She launched into pages of her views about, first of all, capitalism.

MANIFESTO (WASHINGTON, 1965)

"We live in a world which buys and sells everything—in which dollars are measures of value …all are wittingly or unwittingly governed by it—all but those who persistently and vigorously oppose this standard and continually root it out of their lives."

She rejected everything in conventional society—having money, making people my age stay in school when they were ready to take up their place in society (and maybe on the barricades). "In my own married life, I followed the common pattern of turning my resentment of being enslaved by the dollar into an occasion for warfare instead of recognizing it for what it was and learning by practice how a person frees himself from this wretched state."

I still can't tell if she was saying she should earn and manage her own money, or that truly enlightened people should discover in some magical way how to do without it. She seemed to forget that she had just tried to convince me to come out to California to investigate their superior system of higher education, and turned to criticizing the whole assumption that people my age would go to college. "You, as a teen-ager, are nearly grown and ready for an independent life, but our competitive economy does not have a place for you; you must remain dependent on your family and beholden to them, and have no chance to find out through trial-and-error just what you and other people and this world are really like. In families like yours—middle-class and up—your 'job' is to go to school. Your 'product' is good marks, right at this time when you have a lot of positive, creative energy—the very explosive source of revolutionary power throughout history—and in its blind way the adult world recognizes this and knows it must keep you down."

Somehow talk of money veered into the topic of sex. Some of it seemed personal, some of it more like a lecture to someone who needed correction and instruction, and there were many pages on this subject. Was she still trying to work these things out for herself? Was she recalling the dangers to which my older sister and I had been exposed on her watch? Because, despite the fact that I had no boyfriend, and the reality that no one in my life actually cared about me, the problem of sex had faded dramatically since my mother left. It had been in her house that I had watched her lovers come and go, and got in over my head in ill-advised and unsupervised encounters of my own. It had been one of her own boyfriends who had propositioned me and whose side she'd taken against mine.

She mentioned that boyfriend in this letter, explaining the ways in which she had once been, but no longer was, confused. She would not now agree to have sex with someone just because he wouldn't stop pressuring her, nor would she worry about whether her rejection might hurt his feelings.

She was also outraged by the idea of contraception. "I feel it an insult to my very being to put some foreign mechanical article into my body or ingest some chemical that is going to further alter my already delicately-balanced, half-alive nervous and glandular responses, to prevent an act of love from resulting in new life." What she was now in favor of was abstinence. Maybe. Or sexual activities that don't involve intercourse; except, she reflected bitterly, that men never accept that. This was much more than I wanted to know about my mother's sex life.

At this point in the letter she backed herself into a rhetorical corner, where she had to address something that actually did have to do with our relationship—the problem of children. "To have a child is no light matter; you cannot hold someone's love by giving him or her a child, but a child should be the outcome of great love between two people who decide that they want to have a child and raise the child together—and how can anyone make such a decision, to share in caring for a new life, unless they know already by doing it that they can care for themselves?" I doubted that I or any of my sisters had come into being as a result of this kind of great love and considered planning, and had too often heard her say unapologetically (back when she was still my mother) that she could not take care of herself.

"It's easy enough to see that it's done all the time—what people hide is that it is terrible, it destroys them, and it destroys the children. That is, as you have seen, not so hot from the child's point of view." I must have been startled to recognize that she seemed to be considering my position in this narrative.

"I used to think, 'Oh well, flowers scatter their seeds on the wind, fish leave their eggs and spawn and go off never knowing what happened, turtles bury their eggs—life demands more life and children do grow'—in other words, 'I'm not responsible.'"

That's what she thought? She didn't think, she just hoped—hoped, when we were babies, and hoped again, when she left, that we could survive without her?

"But of course we are responsible when we create life, we can't turn ourselves into flowers or fish, we are human beings. And that very refusal to be responsible, in my life, has directly led to my constant unhappiness, suicidal wishes, and resulting willful irresponsibility. Of course I was ignorant, uneducated, undeveloped—and I still am—it is not any easier, but rather, harder all the time to see how I am ever going to become myself and act on my own behalf in my lifetime. I will leave, I suppose, traces of what I might have been, as well as my mistakes, behind me when I die, but not a life of which I'll be able to feel proud."

Was she saying that she now, finally, felt responsible? Maybe she was sorry, but not for me. She hated the world and herself, trapped between a dream of freedom and the incontrovertible truth that she could not take care of herself or anyone else.

What she said about burying eggs and moving on is, of course, true. The Green Turtle, for example (common to Southern California), nests several times a year, leaving behind a hundred or more eggs that hatch without her help. But here's the thing—on average, only about one in a thousand hatchlings makes it to adulthood.

This letter still makes no sense as a letter from mother to daughter. It was perhaps a kind of rhetorical essay, exploring her thoughts and feelings and beliefs on a wide-ranging set of issues, the story that either she or Patti made up serving as a jumping-off point, a way to point out everything wrong with the world.

Or maybe I actually was her intended audience? Maybe cozying up to Patti to gang up on me energized her, got her fired up to compose a lecture, a scolding for me and my unenlightened family.

I didn't want to know any of this. Even three years after our separation, the only thing I cared about was whether or not she was still my mother in any way. For all the times I had asked myself, "Why did she—? What was she thinking when—?" I still clung to the fantasy that she *was* a mother, recalling every instance of affection or nurture—reading books to us, teaching us songs, buying art supplies, taking us to family camp and dance lessons—as if they represented her true self. Those maternal qualities, having been set aside for some terrible reason, might still re-emerge if I could only find some way to restore an alliance with her.

She wrote again six weeks later, this time just a single small sheet, mentioning her plan to save money: "OK, as of today I have in the bank the magnificent sum of $105.00, which as I have just found out by calling the Santa Fe R.R., will more than pay for 1/2 the round trip coach between here and there."

Things were difficult for her at the moment: "Marina can't sleep & and I can't sleep & the grocery store was robbed and Hank has new hours at work and I just got some rejected poems back, I can hardly stand it." In closing, she prodded for an answer to her invitation: "Hope nothing is wrong where you are; almost called Saturday but financial discretion prevailed!"

I don't recall what I wrote in return, but I do have the letter she wrote a week later. Again a single sheet, but with a somewhat different tone. "I'm certainly sorry the gossip I relayed distressed you. I only know of one way to allay fears aroused by rumor, and that is to try to find out the facts—but of course in my anxiety I did not consider your feelings."

From lecturing me in September she reversed course to comment on my older sister: "To tell the truth I guess I got the impression that Patti got her story from you …she might well have made the whole thing up. I wish I knew by now how to resist this kind of thing from her and others like that—it is no help to such people, to be always taken in." Now it became clearer that the two of them had been siding against me weeks earlier, and that the long rant of the September letter had been meant to inform me of the error of my ways (and those of "families like yours"). Now, I was her ally, Patti one of "such people," and she wondered how she could have believed the story about me.

"I could not imagine the situation being the way she described it, without postulating that I just did not know you. But you are great to remind me that I should not repeat unkind gossip in any case, and I certainly will try to be more level-headed if (God forbid!) such nonsense should occur again."

She felt bad about Patti, flirted briefly with a feeling of responsibility, then swerved away from that uncomfortable position, noting that she and Patti were no longer in touch. "I do think it's terrible what has happened to her life and feel terribly the weight of guilt for my ignorant life that allowed it. Yet goodness knows pity and mollycoddling really help no one—whatever her history. Patti alone can take charge of herself and her own life. I have not heard from her in some time."

At this point she hinted that her relationship with Bukowski might not be working out. "My life here is in an uproar. I want to move to a smaller, separate apartment or housekeeping room with Marina but it is hard to go about finding a suitable, inexpensive place—to get out in the daytime with Marina often & long enough to look, when she is used to sleeping all day." It still annoys me to read how she blamed the baby. The one thing that never changed in my life with her was that she absolutely refused to keep the hours the rest of us needed—especially in the months before and after the marriage ended, she was often up until close to dawn, sleeping until mid-afternoon, hurt and angry at any protest.

Later in life she would say, about the end of her life with Bukowski, "Two crazy people just can't live together." (She might, I thought, have learned that lesson during her marriage.) The situation wasn't working for Bukowski, either. In his letters and stories it seems that while he'd loved my mother once (and would love their daughter the rest of his life) he was the one who couldn't live with her, or at least not with her workshops and causes and comrades and meetings, people hanging out at his place talking when he came back from his night job at the post office. In a letter to Henry Miller he wrote, "She's got to constantly correct me, no matter what the hell I say. I can wake up in the morning and say, 'God it's hot.' and she'll say, 'You just think it's hot. It's not as hot as yesterday. Suppose you were in Africa…' this sort of thing." That still sounds exactly like my mother.

Another letter arrived in December. She seemed to pull away from the back-biting adventure she had gotten into with Patti, and apologized again. "I have the awfullest feeling I wrote you a rotten letter... I love both you and Pat very much and why I sometimes act as if there were 'sides' to take, and knock one of you to the other, I can't imagine. If I said anything about Pat or anything that bothered you—I wish it unsaid, that's all I can say."

My mother enjoyed gossiping with any ally, no matter how temporary, about someone else. She needed to feel superior, and I can see how that attitude instilled in me and my sisters a reflexive antagonism toward each other. I wonder how much that unmoderated rivalry, even more than geography, prevented us from being close as we grew up, and for too many years thereafter.

She had a new address. I know now that 5526 Carlton Way was only a few blocks from DeLongpre Avenue, and that Bukowski had helped her find something close by so that he might be part of Marina's life. But all my mother said was, "We have a lovely room here and everything is working out very well—only I dream of financial independence, yet fear it and find excuses to fail to plan for it or fail to carry out my plans. Well, that's all the same old story. As part of my plan is to get enough sleep for a change, I won't sit up writing you."

Perhaps she was not entirely wrong about seeds and turtles and life finding a way. After all, I'm still here, and have a life most would say is well-provisioned and even meaningful. But my oldest sister has, after much mistreatment and too many losses, withdrawn from life, and my youngest sister died, much too young. It was her heart.

In the next generation there are eleven grandchildren, of whom eight are still living. Not a spectacular survival rate, but I have to give her this much: better than turtles.

MARCH ON WASHINGTON
(WASHINGTON, 1965)

The split-level was quiet and empty when I got home from the bus stop, which meant I could listen to the radio. At four o'clock, the local station was broadcasting pop music, and I heard the opening chords of "Do You Want to Know a Secret." I had a friend again, and she was crazy for the Beatles, so I knew most of the words and could sing along. I kept the volume low so that I'd be able to hear my stepmother's sedan when she pulled into the driveway. The living room was still unfurnished, except for the yellow plastic Parsons table that held the radio. My sisters and I weren't supposed to walk on the off-white wall-to-wall carpeting, but with no one to see me, I sat on the window seat and looked out into the small backyard. When the telephone rang I was startled out of whatever daydream may have been developing. After three rings I realized no one else was there to answer it, snapped the radio off, went to the kitchen, and picked up the beige receiver from the wall phone. It didn't occur to me that the call might be for me.

"It's Marcie!" a vaguely familiar voice squealed. *Marcie?* I didn't know any Marcie, but this person seemed to know me. "Marcie! From Ann Arbor!"

A picture began to come into focus—frizzy blonde hair, round face, blue eyes, freckles—and then I did remember. Marcie and I had been in the Unitarian youth group together; she had always been squealing or laughing, or both at the same time, and I had liked her, a lot. And then forgotten her. I had no idea how she had our telephone number; I hadn't heard from anyone in Michigan in a long time, and sometime during the three years and four moves I'd stopped sending anyone another new address.

"We're coming to Washington! For the protest march!" I didn't know what she was talking about, but could tell she assumed I knew all about it. She and her mother would be traveling with a group from Ann Arbor to Washington to protest the war. "You're going to the march, right?"

A long time ago, I was in a youth group where we talked about things like civil rights and nuclear tests and bad wars. At church and at school back in Ann Arbor I would certainly have heard a lot about Vietnam, and by now I might even have been part of a group planning a protest. But in my current life there was no such thing, and Marcie's invitation put me on the spot. I was quick to pretend that I knew which side she was on, and of what, and why, but it was an uneasy pretense. My life was so limited that I simply couldn't reflect on what would be the right position to hold about big public questions. Mostly I kept my profile low, and having any kind of opinion threatened to attract the wrong kind of attention.

"Um, when is it going to be?" I twisted the telephone cord around my fingers.

"It's next month—the week after Thanksgiving. Can you go with us? And can we stay at your house?"

Both were impossible questions. I told her I'd see if I could get permission, and she said she'd call again the next day. I knew without asking that no one could come to stay with us. But maybe, I thought, I might be able to join Marcie and her mother for the march. I didn't know much about the war and why the government kept saying that it was necessary and right, or why so many people seemed to feel the opposite. I knew my mother would be against the war, and going on a protest march was exactly the kind of thing she would do; but she was far away, in another life. I could hardly remember feeling part of something bigger than myself, along with my mother, on the same side. I was trying to figure out who I could be in this new life, to discern what my father (whom I feared) and my stepmother (whom I hardly knew) expected of me. The little identity I had was organized around what I was *not*—not like my mother, not like my older sister.

The truth was, I didn't care about the war. Here's what I cared about: I'd have liked to see someone from my past, someone who'd known me more than six months. I wanted to spend time with Marcie's sweet mother, who had been friendly with mine and always glad to have me and Marcie do our homework in her kitchen. Suddenly, I desperately wanted to get out of the house; to see Marcie, to go the march, to be with people who would talk to me.

I went down to my room, sat on the bed and thought about how to tell my father about the call. Maybe he would remember Marcie's family, and then he'd let me go with them. I pulled up the orange madras bedspread, reached for my book bag, and took out the notebook that M. Boulanger insisted we call a *cahier*. I liked the black-and-white marbled cover and the turquoise ink I'd been using lately. It was like Nanny's, even though there was no version of my ever-changing handwriting that would ever be as beautiful as her perfect cursive. (Now that we'd moved back from New York and saw Nanny often, it was again safe to think about her.)

French was easy. I'd had a good teacher back in New York, and my friend Cecilia and I used to speak French together when we were walking around town or taking an occasional train ride into the city. But it was hard to concentrate on *le vocabulaire* that afternoon. First I was thinking about Cecilia and her house across the street from ours; the deep front porch, her affectionate parents. About how, when her big brother was home, I'd bring over my guitar and we'd all sing. He and I knew a lot of the same songs, and I taught Cecilia harmonies to "Banks of the Ohio" and "Maid of Constant Sorrow," and we sang together the way I once had with my sister and mother. Then I was remembering autumn just a year ago, walking with Cecilia through fallen leaves and talking about how pretty the scene was and how I might paint it, or what she might write about it. Then I was even further back, in Ann Arbor, looking down from a classroom window into the University School courtyard, seeing the gray afternoon light suddenly become blue as the first snow of the year began to fall. And then I stopped.

There was a baffling (if lifesaving) disconnect between how I was seen and treated by my parents and how other adults seemed to regard me. In Hastings, my tenth-grade English teacher asked me how I felt about getting a stepmother, and said I was "very mature" when I explained that I planned to get along with her for the sake of my little sisters. When he realized none of us were going to our father's wedding and that we did not know the woman he was marrying, the teacher had been taken aback. Uneasy, I worried that I had said too much, failed to convey that I had a good, respectable family and that my sisters and I were all truly better off with our father.

THE GOOD POETIC MOTHER

In Bethesda, another English teacher saw I was completely at sea when it came to interpreting literature, and tried to show me how a book could be about one thing and also mean something more. We read *The Scarlet Letter* and *The Crucible*, and Mrs. Lechliter was the first person I'd heard mention Joseph McCarthy's witch hunts, or the House Un-American Activities Committee, since my mother left. I tried to convey a cautious sympathy with what I divined were her views. I understood that she couldn't talk directly about her own politics, but when she mentioned that her husband had lost his State Department job because of "Low-Blow Joe," I felt we might have a bond.

Dinner was at 6:30. My stepmother always prepared an evening meal, although I thought she wasn't all that crazy about cooking. That night we had Swiss steak and rice and canned peas and I was glad it wasn't liver because that was the only thing I really could not get down. The last time we'd had it I had to leave the table and was in trouble for days. If Sara and Ruthie bickered then they weren't allowed to talk at all and we ate in silence except for reminders not to put elbows on the table, or our father expounding on his successes at work. I was relieved when I could get up and start to clear the table.

After dinner I washed and dried the dishes, scrubbed the stainless steel sink and swept the tiled floor. I hung up the damp dishtowel and walked quietly up to my father's study. He sat at his mahogany desk, the sleeves of his white shirt rolled up, reading some papers from work and making notes with a black fountain pen. He looked up impatiently when I knocked on the door jamb, peering over his reading glasses. I didn't do a very good job of explaining what I wanted, and I knew his answer before I finished talking about the war and the march and our old friends. He either didn't remember

MARCH ON WASHINGTON (WASHINGTON, 1965)

Marcie's family, or hadn't really liked them, and he was not moved by anything I said.

"No, it's not safe." And, "What good do you think that's going to do?" And, "Are you trying to be like your mother?" And, "No, you can't go." It was what I had expected, after all. I wasn't shocked, and even had a little nerve left. I had a right to ask, didn't I?

"Well, what do you think about Vietnam? Are you against the war or for it?"

He stared at me for a long moment. "That's above my pay grade."

When I still had a mother, I had walked a picket line with her. In the final year we were together, she sometimes dressed all in black, and said she planned to do that until the end of the Vietnam War. But by then I was embarrassed not only by the black shirt but the fact that she didn't wear a bra under it, and infuriated by the contrast between the energy and concern she put into political protest and the limited attention she had for her daughters. Once she left, I scoffed when she wrote of going down to the Air Force base to get arrested, and I was glad she was so far away. I didn't go to the 1965 antiwar march or any of the other demonstrations during the war that so defined my generation. All of that was above my pay grade.

FAILURE TO LAUNCH (TEXAS, 1967)

It takes just over two seconds to fall eighty feet. The climb from the sandy beach at the edge of Hamilton Pool—a swimming hole near Dripping Springs, Texas—to the rocky overhang above cold, green water probably took five minutes. Once I saw the path end abruptly at the edge of the cliff, and maybe looked down to make sure there were no outcroppings to break my fall, I didn't hesitate.

There was no "failure to launch" in 1967, only failure. Flunked out. Messed up. Blew it. Either stupid or lazy, but in any case failed. After the educational and relational discontinuities of my secondary school years I had probably not been ready to go away to college, but the concept of a gap year had not come into being yet. A high school senior was either college-bound or not, and the only thing I understood even less than higher education was the world of work.

The University of Texas, fifteen hundred miles away in a state I'd visited only once, had not been a terribly logical choice either. I'd been accepted at my state school, but the expanding University of Maryland had a housing shortage in the fall of 1966. I could enroll, but I'd have to live at home for at least the first year, and for reasons that I intuited but were never spelled out, that wasn't going to be an option. I didn't drive, because my parents would have had to pay more for car insurance if they let me use their car. Either there wasn't enough money, or I wasn't worth spending money on, and maybe I didn't want to know which.

The other reason, which I didn't know until after I left home, was that they were planning to move from the four-bedroom split-level house to a two-bedroom apartment. Neither my father or stepmother particularly liked having a house and a yard; I'd been in charge of mowing the lawn for the past two summers, and maybe Sara, at eleven, was too young to take up yard work. The other thing I didn't know was that my stepmother was pregnant.

What college options had I really considered? My classmates seemed either to know how to choose a college (and then get into it), or they had parents interested in helping them, but I don't recall any discussions in my house about what might be best for me. My mother had by then revealed her antipathy for higher education, considering it just another way for conventional society to keep young people entrained in a repressive value system.

I was on my own, with a copy of the telephone book-sized *Barron's Guide* and little idea of how to make use of it. What was the difference between Washington College and George Washington University? Between Eastern Michigan and the University of Michigan? I remember looking at the columns for tuition and fees, and at some point hit on the University of Texas. Rich in oil and gas holdings, UT had tuition so low that the rate for out-of-state students was lower than the University of Maryland's in-state cost. I could explain, if anyone wondered why I was going so far away, that it would be cheaper to go to Texas than to Maryland.

Another motivation, even if not fully conscious, was probably that this was the school my stepmother had attended, where she had been one of the first women to work for the student newspaper, and had become the Phi Beta Kappa girl who had so impressed my father. This choice would be hard for them to disapprove. I floated the idea, got a somewhat interested response, and by the spring of 1966 it was decided that I was going to Texas in the fall.

Eighteen girls lived in Shangri-La Women's Co-Op, one of six two-story duplexes with similarly-utopian names arranged around a grassy square. My stepmother's younger sister, only a year older than I, lived in Valhalla; it was she who picked me up at the airport and drove me to campus.

The temperature was in the high nineties as I hauled my suitcases past bike racks and found my name on a list taped to the front door. "Room C" was printed next to my name, along with a penciled note: *Turn left, up the stairs, door on the left at the end of the hall!* The note seemed friendly even if the house was empty. The corner room was already decorated entirely in white cotton eyelet—curtains, skirts on both desks, coverlets on the beds. My new roommate, I would learn, had transferred from a two-year bible college near her hometown. I sat at one of the desks, unsure which my invisible roommate had already picked for herself, and how much of the closet I might use.

Despite that lonely beginning, the co-op turned out to be a good fit. The houses were each managed by a student coordinator and run by the residents, with clear rules and expectations. There was a specified way to vacuum the common room, directions for exactly how and with what detergent to mop the kitchen floor, a schedule for which menus would be prepared when and a book of recipes to follow. The pantry was always stocked, I didn't have to pretend to already know what I was supposed to do, and, for the first months at least, I liked

FAILURE TO LAUNCH (TEXAS, 1967)

Austin and being in college. The fact that people spoke so differently was not a barrier; after a few weeks, classmates stopped telling me that I sounded like a Yankee. That adaptability was second nature, and without any deliberate effort my Midwestern/Mid-Atlantic accent was overridden by a Texas twang.

I knew that I was supposed to find a job. Or had my father said it could wait until second semester? But in any case this is where I first fell down. I was shy and self-conscious, didn't know what "work-study" meant, and couldn't bring myself to enter into a conversation that might reveal how much I didn't understand. Even after I somehow found a part-time job—it involved filing and some typing—I let it slip away. The office manager had asked me to bring her my class schedule next time I came to the office, and then I forgot when I was supposed to go back, and then I was too embarrassed to show up again.

There was no question of going home for holidays. I spent Thanksgiving with a housemate who lived in Galveston, then Christmas with my stepmother's family in a small town about forty miles from Austin. They were friendly and made room for me in their modest house, but didn't know what to make of me any more than I knew them. It was awkward and lonely and I felt ungrateful not to appreciate their kindness more.

Things began to slip sometime after Christmas. I started spending time with a group of similarly-unfocused friends—drinking beer, playing folk music, staying out late—and by spring I was missing more classes than I attended. I didn't reflect on what was happening to me, and had no inkling that, four years after losing my mother and after too many months away from what family I had left, I was becoming depressed.

THE GOOD POETIC MOTHER

The on-campus women's co-ops still had curfews and parietal rules (no men upstairs, no "public displays of affection" in the common room) but students over eighteen could stay out late, even all night if they left word where they'd be. By January, along with someone whose name I no longer remember (definitely *not* my quiet, religious roommate), I was routinely signing myself out to a boys' dorm two blocks away, always bringing along my guitar. I remember the boy who taught me Buffy Sainte-Marie's "Universal Soldier," who was so admiring of my guitar-playing that I forgave him for leaving a cigarette balanced over the sound hole (the pale spruce top still shows that burn mark). Although completely unsupervised, we didn't get into much trouble. It was risky to have beer in the dorm, and the most daring adventure I recall was the night we all ate morning glory seeds. They were supposed to get us high, like smoking banana peels (which we didn't believe) or eating peyote buttons (which we couldn't get). I remember how huge my pupils were and that I was the only one who didn't throw up, and that later, after someone read about the pesticides used to coat the seeds, we gave up on that experiment.

A second Delta flight to Washington had run out of standby seats. I dragged my duffel bag across the terrazzo floor of Atlanta's new "Jet Age" terminal to the pay phones, dropped in a dime and retrieved it as soon as the collect call was accepted. "I got bumped again. The next flight's at two, so I'll be at National around four. I hope." I pocketed the dime, ashamed to tell my parents that I had so little money with me. It was going to be a long, hungry day.

After eight months away, I was coming home to Bethesda for spring vacation, seeing for the first time the apartment where my father and stepmother and two sisters now lived. I flew on a half-price ticket, so my stepmother had no financial arguments against the trip. In any case, she seemed happier that spring, pregnant with her own baby at last and expecting that I would be back home briefly and temporarily. The apartment was crowded, but I could sleep in the den, for the week.

When I arrived at dinner time, my father told me that Nanny was in the hospital. She'd had a heart attack, but would be fine. No, I couldn't visit; she was still weak, hooked up to tubes and monitors. "You don't want to see her like that. Maybe later in the week."

She had a second attack late that night, and was dead by morning.

The loss meant different things to each person in the family, of course. My father said that at least he'd made peace with his mother, as he never had with his father. My stepmother was genuinely distraught, and said later that Nanny had been the only person she could talk to about my father without feeling disloyal. I had lost the one person who loved me.

Over the next few days we went to the hospital to pick up Nanny's things, to Gawler's Funeral Home, to a pretty church that none of us had ever attended, and then I was back in Texas. I cried once. The boy I was with that day didn't think my grandmother's death could be the reason, said I'd just had too much beer. I wasn't sure if he was right or not. I didn't really grasp how alone I was.

I talked to my mother on the phone; it was my first conversation with her since high school. She didn't have much to say about Nanny, although at the beginning of the conversation I thought she was trying not to cry, but she had some advice for me. I should "drop out," she thought, and she didn't mean just out of college. "Lots of people are doing that now. Just refusing to go along with all the bullshit. The war, the bosses. You should do that." She was still in Los Angeles, living on welfare, separated from Bukowski, quite dropped out herself. Later on, I would tell the story of this exchange with bitter humor, but it wasn't funny then.

Two weeks after returning to school I went with a few girls from the co-op to the swimming hole thirty miles west of Austin. We parked at the edge of Texas Route 962 and hiked down a steep path to a narrow beach shaded by overhanging rock, across the "bottomless" pool from a fifty-foot waterfall. Cliff swallows nested among stalactites, and maidenhair ferns grew around boulders near the splashing water.

We picnicked on the sandy shore, reminiscing about the school year that was coming to an end, sneaking some Lone Star beer, and pretending not to watch the boys' horseplay on the other side of the collapsed grotto. Every few minutes one of them, egged on by the others, climbed up the hidden path to a cliff above the waterfall. Then a running jump and an eighty-foot drop, legs churning to a spectacular cannonball. The boys cheered wildly; we rolled our eyes.

And then I slipped away from the group, climbed the cliff, and walked off the edge without a pause. My friends were shocked but impressed, and as soon as I could speak again I said I was fine. Just the breath knocked out of me. No, I didn't know what got into me. Maybe the Lone Star.

The next day I hobbled to the health center for an x-ray, and they kept me there. When my father called to tell me that my second half-sister, his fifth daughter, had been born, he chewed out the unlucky girl who answered the house phone, because he hadn't been told I was in the infirmary. I couldn't explain to him or anyone else what had happened.

I somehow found my way back to my philosophy class, sat in the back row of the lecture hall long enough to find out the assignment and somehow—I don't know how—wrote a term paper on "Humanistic Ethics." I got a C in that class and Fs in everything else, and was on scholastic probation by the time I came home in a back brace, my x-rays in an envelope.

Seventeen years later, after an early marriage and divorce followed by a happier second marriage, sudden widowhood, and a breakdown at least as serious as the one I'd had in college, I told the story of the bottomless swimming hole and the eighty-foot cliff to a therapist. It seemed to me an amusing account of uncharacteristically irresponsible risk-taking, and I was surprised when the kind and worried doctor said, "That's the kind of thing we call a suicidal gesture."

TRANSCRIPT OF RECORD (WASHINGTON, 1968)

It had been raining since my mother arrived in Washington from Los Angeles, but she was determined to go down to the Mall to see Resurrection City, in solidarity with the Poor People's Campaign. I had agreed to come along, in some kind of solidarity with *her*, but regretted it as soon as we got off the bus on Constitution Avenue. We walked through what was left of the sodden grass, past the reflecting pool, to a dreary shantytown. The lean-tos and tents were almost afloat in mud, with duckboard walkways around and through a maze of haphazard temporary shelters. There was nothing happening—no speeches, no singing, no meetings—but my mother was undaunted. She'd be in town a few more days, and planned to come back to the tent city when things dried out a bit. In the end, the protesters were evicted and the camp demolished before anything could dry out, and by the end of June all traces of Resurrection City were gone.

Looking back, I'm struck by what a dark time that was. The Tet offensive in Vietnam began at the end of January, 1968, and at the end of March President Lyndon Johnson, as tired of the war as anyone, announced that he would not seek re-election. Martin Luther King was murdered on April 4 in Memphis, and the riots in Washington went on for four days after that. I could see smoke rising above 14th and U Streets from as far away as the suburban apartment where I'd been living with my parents since coming back from Texas. Bobby Kennedy was killed on June 5, and that trek to Resurrection City was the last time I would see my mother for another thirteen years.

That spring was also when I met a young man whose chance advice would change the course of my life. Wilbur Cohen, the Ann Arbor friend who got my father his Washington job in the early sixties, became a cabinet secretary in 1968, heading the department in which, extremely far down the line, I was working as a clerk-typist. Employees were given the afternoon off if they wanted to attend the swearing-in of the new department chief; my father and stepmother were planning to attend, and they would give me a ride downtown. By the end of the ceremony I had someone else to ride with, and somewhere else to go—the three Cohen boys were at the event, and the youngest one, at least, remembered me from Michigan. They invited me along when they went back to their rambling suburban house, where Mrs. Cohen seemed glad to see me, and for the next few weeks I spent a lot of time with those nice boys and their friends.

I'm not sure how I explained why, at nineteen, I wasn't in college. One of those young men (and I wish I could remember his name now) pointed out the obvious fact that working and paying rent to my parents and buying a savings bond every pay period wasn't ever going to make it possible to go back to school. He had a better idea—his mother had left college for marriage, and when the marriage ended and she was left with no degree and limited prospects, she took a job at a local college because their employees could take courses free. She had worked until she finished her B.A.—he didn't say how long it took her, and I didn't ask.

By the end of the summer I had applied to George Washington University as a transfer student, and had a job working as a transcript clerk in the registrar's office. Under the direction of a thin-lipped, exacting spinster named Eleanor, I checked and updated students' official transcripts of record. My own transcript, however, was a stumbling block. Because of being on scholastic probation when I left Texas, I could not take courses for credit. But, since I already worked at the university, I could audit a class if I wanted to.

I became a regular at the admissions office, finding out from someone there how to navigate this dilemma, what form to fill out to get permission to audit a course. I'd already decided on second semester Spanish, maybe because the best first-semester grade I'd gotten at Texas had been in Spanish. My admission was only for the fall semester; I'd have to petition again in the spring for permission to audit another class.

There was only one right way to update a transcript, and that was Eleanor's way. Long before word processors or desktop computers, grades were printed each semester by a mechanical posting machine on oversized sheets of off-white cardstock that became, physically as well as bureaucratically, a student's "permanent record." Transcript requests came in the mail and over the counter, and those request slips went to the file room clerks, who, in this monastic corner of the university bureaucracy, were the only ones permitted to remove or replace student record folders. Every morning, a stack of paper-stuffed file jackets was delivered to my gray metal desk. One of Eleanor's rules was that I could not have more than one file open at a time, and as I think back to the sheaves of flimsy carbons, half-page advisor approval notes, and dozens of drop-add slips a folder might contain, I appreciate her reasoning.

The job mostly involved checking. Was the permanent record correct? Did the courses and grades posted for each semester match the separate grade slips? Was the student's status, major, and personal information accurate? And most important, was the student record "encumbered"? An overdue library book, an unpaid fee or meal plan invoice meant the transcript would not be issued until the student's account was paid. I felt bad when I had to turn back a transcript request, and took it as a cautionary tale.

I was intimidated by Eleanor, and more than willing to do exactly as she said. I did well with rules, grateful for the structure and safety that clear guidelines represented, believing that was the path to a life more stable than I'd had before. I had been ashamed of my mother even in the years when I had loved her, and then terrified as she, and as a consequence my own life, came inexorably apart during our final year together. For all the shock and grief of her departure and the lonely, unloved life with my father, I never wanted to risk that kind of insecurity again.

My Spanish class met twice a week, from five-thirty to seven. Eleanor had made it clear that I needed to stay at my desk until five, but as soon as she covered her typewriter I grabbed my sweater and notebook and dashed down the steps of Rice Hall. As I passed Red Lion Row, the aroma from Mrs. Chang's stopped me for a minute. *It's only ten after five—maybe an egg roll? I can eat it on my way to class.* The egg roll was almost too hot to eat, and without sauce tasted mostly of grease. I was still wiping my fingers when I got to the townhouse on G Street and found Señora Somebody's class in a crowded former parlor.

THE GOOD POETIC MOTHER

She had us introduce ourselves in Spanish, and I could remember enough to say, "Mi nombre es Irène," pronouncing it like *eee-wren*. We took turns reading a dialogue from the text book and I was relieved to understand most of it.

I approached the instructor's desk at the end of class. "I'm auditing your class this fall."

She gave me a friendly smile. "¿Oh? ¿*Por que*? You seem to be prepared for this class."

I had to explain that I worked in the registrar's office and that meant I could audit a class at no cost. But I wanted to eventually work toward a degree, and needed to find a way to show that I could do better than I had at Texas, two years earlier.

"If I take the quizzes and do the homework and take the final, do you think you could write a note saying what grade I'd have gotten? If I were a regular student?" She definitely didn't have to do this, I knew.

"Well—" She stopped for a moment, thinking. "I don't see why not." (I wish so much, now, that I could remember her name as well as her kindness.)

After taking the final exam, I brought the instructor's note to the admissions office. I filled out the request to enroll in Introduction to American Literature, and a few days later was allowed to register.

By 1969 the memory of Resurrection City had faded a bit, and early in the year I wrote to my mother to give her news of my life. I assumed she'd be relieved, maybe even proud, to hear that I was working and going to school, had my own apartment and a steady boyfriend. I certainly assumed she'd be pleased to know I was "very happy—secure, confidant, enthusiastic, optimistic—feeling better about myself than ever before." I did not receive a reply.

TRANSCRIPT OF RECORD (WASHINGTON, 1968)

College English was harder than I expected—not the reading, which had been my favorite thing since first grade, but "interpreting" the assigned stories and essays. It made me nervous—how could we know for sure what the author *meant?* But I liked the instructor and by the end of the semester was no longer too shy to offer my own ideas during class discussion, and my quiz and essay grades had improved. In late May I brought my grade report to the admissions office and filled out another petition, and by the end of the week it had been signed. I wasn't a degree candidate yet, but now I could keep taking classes for credit without having to seek permission every semester.

I wrote to my mother again in September, describing how being on a college campus gave me the energized feeling that fall is really the beginning of the year, and telling her that I'd been promoted at work. I asked how she was and how her life was going, said I'd love to hear from her.

I finally got a letter in November. Her life was in disarray. She had moved from Los Angeles to San Francisco, hoping that she and four-year-old Marina could live with Patti, but that had apparently been a disappointment. Together they had three children under five years of age, and I imagined that Patti was no longer willing to take care of any more children in order to make our mother's life more manageable.

Something my mother wrote in her 1961 journal, before the end of the marriage but during the time my father was already in Washington, helps me to better understand my older sister's premature departure from the family. Patti had just turned sixteen when my mother wrote this:

THE GOOD POETIC MOTHER

June 9, 1961.

    It's raining hard and Patti overslept (so did I but that's usual) and is downstairs doing a wash and sorting laundry because the kids don't have any clothes.

Frances Dean Smith (Journal)

Now, eight years after that rainy day in Ann Arbor, she wrote to me that she had been "confused and unhappy in San Francisco, knowing that the life I had expected and planned was not going to work, but not facing it. When I got your letter I was so happy to hear from you I sat down to answer right away but my letter just went on and on without saying anything and finally I put it aside while I tried to 'get myself together' and come to grips with the situation. I threw it away when I packed and now here it is weeks away from then."

I don't know what I felt when I read all this. Dismay? Disappointment? Chagrin? Her state of mind seemed so similar to what it had been when we'd last lived together. Perhaps I was sorry for her. I may even have wondered if there was anything I might do to help her.

Well, yes, there was.

"And the main thing I want to say is, <u>I want to see you</u>. Will you come out and visit us for a while? I will be living in a rented trailer fairly near the beach until June. It seems to me it has been a very long time since you have been in California; you ought to try it before you settle down in the East. I do so very much want to see you and be with you. I hope you will at least consider it. <u>Please come</u>. Try to come before Christmas. If that is impossible, let me know when you think you can come and how much money you will need. Though I still don't have a job, I do have a home and a stable future and so—please come! If you don't like to be idle and penniless, you can certainly get a job out here. Then again if you want to live free for a while, this is the perfect setup. Either way, give it a try. Come and see me ...and please write soon even if you can't decide right away! Much love to you—Mama."

I must have recognized the desperation in her repeated entreaties. Perhaps I tried not to take in the clear evidence that she thought of me now, and invited me again, only because she had given up on Patti. (Patti's third child had died in infancy, her marriage was over; she was using a variety of drugs to dull some of her pain and couldn't take care of anyone else.)

Nothing I'd told my mother of my improved self-esteem and growing self-sufficiency moved her at all, except, perhaps, to make me seem an even better candidate to come out to California and move in with her. I don't know if I answered her letter or not, and I have no evidence of any further correspondence between us for the following decade.

The next semester, spring 1970, I did not register for class, having lost traction somehow, feeling less certain that going to college was really important. Perhaps my fragile self-confidence could not stand up to the weight of my mother's indifference to my academic efforts. I broke up with the boyfriend I'd been with for a year, spent Christmas alone, and perhaps was ready for something different.

There are three statements my father made to me over the course of my life that I have never forgotten. When I came home from the University of Texas in June of 1967, on scholastic probation and with a broken back, he said, "I'm not paying for grades like that." I understood that I was in disgrace, and had accepted his reaction as fair. When, trying to figure out what to do next, I asked him about the Peace Corps (he'd been a senior official there), he told me, "They're not looking for people like you." He was telling me who and what I was, and what I was not.

The third proclamation, in 1970 (after I'd worked for more than three years, lived on my own for two, and had been, until recently, taking college courses at night) was this: "You ought to think about majoring in economics. Being an economist is a good job for a woman in Washington."

I wasn't sure what had gotten his attention; why he took me to lunch that day and gave me what turned out to be, like my friend's suggestion I work at the university, life-changing advice. Perhaps I had let him know I wasn't registered for class that spring, and he was taking my education seriously at a moment when I was losing confidence. This was a vivid contrast both to my mother's wildly impractical exhortation that I join her in a beachside trailer, and to the attitude my father himself had seemed to have had about me for my entire life. I was not at all sure I was smart enough to master economics, but elated at the possibility that he had decided I was. I went to the bookstore that same day, and spent the rest of the spring term reading and taking notes on *Introductory Economics.*

I took the first two semesters of economics that summer, algebra and statistics that fall, trigonometry in the spring, and at the end of that semester I got married. I'm sorry now that I didn't take advantage of a few more years of single and self-sufficient life, but at the time it seemed an obviously good decision. I had met my first husband, a Vietnam veteran, in the registrar's office. He was the night clerk, a friend to everyone, and like me was working his way through school. He played the guitar and we taught each other songs, went to parties and on camping trips with friends of his from a church social club. I think I wanted to become as conventional, as normal, as I possibly could; he seemed a good candidate to help me build that life. We planned and paid for the wedding ourselves; my mother did not attend, and I did not mind. She wouldn't fit into the life I was constructing at all. My husband and I worked and went to school, and, even after our son was born in February, 1974, I kept on taking classes.

Eventually my grades were good enough to provide some fragile support for my self-esteem—an A from an economics or statistics professor probably felt like the approval I'd longed for from my father (and these authority figures were, of course, all men). Bit by bit, my confidence and psyche became stronger, although, at the rate of three or four courses a year, the path to a degree was going to be excruciatingly long.

In the mid-1970s, the university instituted a ninety-semester hour B.A. program, which meant that I could complete a bachelor's degree in the equivalent of three, rather than four, years. Finishing suddenly seemed both doable and completely out of reach. My husband and I might manage without my salary for a year, but the problem of tuition remained—once I quit my university job, classes would no longer be free. I don't remember when I talked to my father about these not-quite-formulated plans, but when, in a rare and ill-considered flush of generosity he offered to pay my tuition for my two remaining semesters, I was amazed and grateful. His willingness to help seemed to undo all the things he'd said before, and to make real the approval I thought I'd given up wanting.

I had resigned from my job and was getting ready to register for fall classes when my father telephoned to tell me (in a familiar tone of irritation and impatience, as if I were responsible for whatever problem he had encountered) that he was not, after all, going to pay my tuition. He had not consulted my stepmother before making that spontaneous offer, and, ten years after dropping out of a master's degree program to marry him and finish raising his children, she was about to enroll in law school. They were going to have other tuition bills to pay.

My husband had his Army discharge money, and I had the savings bonds I'd accumulated during my first year of work. We would live frugally, I would work hard to finish school in as little time as possible, and we could squeak by. We didn't talk about my father.

RUNAWAY MOTHER (CALIFORNIA, 1981)

I was driving down Ashland Avenue for the third time, trying to find my mother. She had been a stranger to me for half my life, and although I was thirty-two years old and had a child of my own, the closer I got to Santa Monica ("Ocean Park," she'd said on the phone; it seemed to be an important distinction) the more I felt like the teenager I'd been when she left. Confused, hurt, and pissed off.

It had been two decades since we last lived together, and during my teens and twenties we had almost no contact. If you'd asked me about her back then I would have said, "I don't know where she is, and that's fine with me. She left me and my three sisters with our father. We're not in touch." If pressed, I'd concede, "Right, I'm the second daughter. How old was I then? Fourteen, and can we change the subject?" I would certainly not mention her one-time lover, the poet Charles Bukowski—let alone their daughter, the little half-sister I barely knew.

I pulled over, left the car at the end of the block and started back down the street on foot. The one-story duplexes had nearly-identical

THE GOOD POETIC MOTHER

white siding, small yards, and cracked concrete walkways, and only the front doors were distinctive in their different colors and varying degrees of dilapidation. Most of the unit numbers were hidden in tumbles of flowering vines, so I counted unmarked doorways and tried to figure out how close I might be.

I had talked myself (or backed myself) into this visit. My life was finally settled down—I'd worked my way through college and graduate school, and through marriage and divorce; I had a steady job and a new husband. Everything was fine, except for the fact—which had become increasingly hard to reconcile with the well-ordered life I'd so carefully constructed—that my mother and I didn't know each other. I was as ready as I could ever be when an opportunity came into view—an economics conference in San Francisco, a paper to present, a travel stipend. I could tell myself that the real reason for the expedition was professional, and that going down to Los Angeles to look for my runaway mother was just a side trip. Armored with hard-won and still-fragile self-confidence, holding my professional paper before me like a shield, I might survive the encounter.

There it was—number 511. The door on the right was marked "B," so the unlabeled one had to be "A." The inner door was open and the screen was patched in a few places with scotch tape. A bowl of water sat on the stoop. *Right, she mentioned a cat.*

"You're not allergic like your father, are you?" she'd asked on the phone. I am, in fact, but I said, "Not very," and since I wouldn't be spending the night and Mama said the cat was mostly outside, I was sure it would be fine.

The room beyond the screen was dark. I tapped on the wooden edge of the door, heard a creak and saw a shape and then—there she was. As she pushed the door toward me, I stepped back, almost tripping. "Oh, Irene! Oh, oh, oh! It's so great to see you!" She held out

RUNAWAY MOTHER (CALIFORNIA, 1981)

her arms, and we hugged briefly. We were the same height. Should I have known that? Her hair was completely gray, pulled back in a long braid, and she was wearing bifocals. That was a surprise. When I got glasses in fifth grade (I'd needed them since third) Mama said she couldn't understand how I could be so nearsighted, since her own vision, like her father's, had always been perfect.

She smelled like cigarettes and coffee and sweat. Why had I imagined she'd quit smoking? Because she always said she hated herself for smoking, that she should quit, that she was trying to, was going to. Soon.

I took in her black canvas Chinese slippers, loose white cotton pants, and a blue-flowered top that looked like one of her old maternity smocks. Her body had become broad and soft, and she didn't seem to be wearing a bra. The bones of her face were less distinct than I remembered, her skin more lined, but I recognized, behind those oversized lenses, her green-flecked hazel eyes.

I wanted to believe I was a good person, but having been left to grow up with my father had, in truth, made me more striving, selfish, approval-seeking, and shallow than I liked to admit. Like him, I tried to get close to people who seemed successful and important, and steer clear of those on the margins—like my mother and the poet she'd taken up with soon after arriving in California. Although I gathered by now that in some circles Charles Bukowski was Somebody, no one I knew had ever heard of him.

"Come in, come in! We've been waiting for you."

We? Yes, there was a tall girl with lots of red hair behind my mother, hanging back, smiling shyly. I knew, of course, that my half-sister would be a teenager by now, but somehow I hadn't thought about her at all as I set out on this unlikely expedition. I noted blue eyes and freckles, and didn't recognize her in the least.

THE GOOD POETIC MOTHER

"Well, come on in. Of course you remember Marina—Marina, here's your big sister, Irene!" Marina and I hugged too, even more briefly. *How could we remember each other? She wasn't even four years old the last time I saw her.*

The three of us stood in what seemed to be a living room, with a couch that was clearly a bed. Mama explained that she slept there so Marina could have the back room, between the kitchen and the rear door. I could see a handful of silverware in a jar of cloudy water on the kitchen countertop, and a sink filled with dishes, and I had the unwanted memory of another kitchen, cigarettes stubbed out on an eggy saucer, and the sour smell of an unwashed cloth. I caught a faint but definite smell of cat pee.

Marina, barefoot in blue jeans and a close-fitting ribbed red sweater, looked like the teenager she was. There was nothing wrong with how she was dressed, but now *I* was suddenly self-conscious about the navy A-line skirt and tailored jacket that I'd bought for the conference. I'd wanted to look nice and thought I did, but now I had the feeling both of them thought I was very strange. My palms were damp.

Mama seemed nervous, too. She glanced toward the kitchen. "Can I get you anything? Would you like some tea? I have another mug around here someplace. Marina, do we have any tea bags left?" Marina looked uncertain and I said I was fine, lowering myself awkwardly to the edge of the couch-bed. The blue-and-purple striped Indian bedspread was frayed at one end where it didn't quite cover a stained pillow. Mama settled with a grunt into a steel-framed black canvas chair and Marina leaned in the kitchen doorway.

This wasn't what I expected. Every surface in the tiny sitting room was covered—books, dishes, magazines—making the space feel even smaller. Believing she had left us in order to achieve a more authentic and mentally-healthy life, I had imagined that such a radical uprooting would have brought her complete satisfaction and peace—and somehow made her a better housekeeper. But this was just a smaller, warm-weather version of the Ann Arbor house—the tenth and final place we had lived together—and the unwelcome memory of a mattress on the floor, an empty refrigerator, dirty dishes and unwashed laundry started to make me feel sad and irritated. I pushed those images away—the whole purpose of this undertaking was to start fresh. No doubt our long separation and my stubborn anger had obscured many of her virtues, and I hoped that being with her would help me begin to reconnect with all that was good in her. I tried to find something that was related in any way to the life we once shared. Did she still have an autoharp? Did they sing? Draw? Searching the small room for some clue, I remembered suddenly that what my mother was sitting on was called a butterfly chair. "Didn't we have a chair like that in Michigan?" I asked.

"Oh, did we?" Vague, then brighter. "Oh, yes, you're right! When we were still living in Ypsilanti. I remember, with an orange canvas cover that your father hated. Now, did we bring that chair when we moved to Ann Arbor? I'm not sure. My memory's so bad. To be honest, I really try not to think about anything to do with that terrible bourgeois town."

My readiness to join in her reminiscences was brought up short. I remembered Lead Belly's "Bourgeois Blues"—it was on the same record as "Goodnight Irene," the song my mother named me for—but the bourgeois town he sang of was racist Washington D.C. in the 1930s and had nothing to do with Michigan.

A bright blue bookcase stood against the wall at the foot of the bed, stuffed with paperbacks, copies of *The New Yorker* and *The Nation*, loose sheets of typing paper, pads and notebooks leaning against each other. There was a pile of newspapers on the floor. "Are you writing a lot of poetry these days?" I felt like an envoy from a foreign land, where diplomatic relations had been suspended for some time and it was no longer clear who was anyone's ally, let alone most-favored-nation.

"Well, I write a lot for a while, then I get bogged down and think I should never write again. But that reminds me, I put some pieces together to give to you, only I can't find them. Marina, what did we do with that folder?"

"Maybe you left it at Beyond Baroque?" Marina offered. (I hadn't heard then of what is now the highly-regarded Beyond Baroque Literary Arts Center in Venice, California. My mother was an original member of a long-running poetry group there, reading her own works and listening to others' poems. She encouraged and mentored many young poets, and after her death was honored in a memorial reading for the center's fortieth anniversary.)

I noticed for the first time how much Marina looked like my other sisters. Which would mean she looked like me, too. I felt a little dizzy.

"Oh, that's right. Too bad." Mama turned toward me with a rueful grimace. "I lose my poems constantly. My friends make sure to save any I give them because they know I can't keep track of things. I don't know where anything is around here, but when I get some money I'm going to look for a used file cabinet and get set up better."

I didn't want to focus on the mess, or start hearing my father's words in my head—"This place is a pigsty." I had come to see if we could be friends.

Maybe this was the right time.

"Well, I actually brought something for you." I reached into my blue canvas briefcase, retrieving the eighty-page typescript I'd copied and bound between stiff beige covers before leaving my office. "I thought you might like to have a copy of my thesis." I had hoped she'd understand how much it meant, be pleased, and maybe even impressed, with my accomplishment. Now, faced with the accumulating evidence of how different we were, I wasn't so sure.

She did not immediately reach for the neatly-fastened pages.

"It was such a huge project, the biggest thing I've ever done. There were so many times I thought I'd never be able to finish it." I was rambling.

After years of my father calling me "Stupid," and my mother only occasionally remembering to say, "He doesn't really mean that" (and later, of course, not being around to say anything), every good grade and every graduation had seemed a miracle. When my master's thesis was accepted I felt it might mean—just possibly—that *I* was acceptable, finally smart enough and competent enough to earn a secure place in the world. Now I was bringing this to her like I once brought projects home from school, always forgetting she wasn't interested in my ability to crayon inside the mimeographed lines. "That's nice," she'd say back then, "but maybe next time you might want to make up your own picture."

I handed her the document, and she turned it over and back again as if not sure which was the front. "Oh, the title page is inside," I said. "I had it bound for you, so you can keep it, if you want to. It's about unemployment, it's what I just gave a talk about in San Francisco. You see, there are lots of reasons for joblessness, and people are out of work for different lengths of time and so you have to look at the turnover patterns, and..."

Her expression remained blank and my words wound down. She nodded, opened the cover and read the first few sentences.

THE GOOD POETIC MOTHER

"Oh, yes, I see. Turnover. Unemployment. Uh huh." She leafed through a few more pages, stopped at one of the tables. "Lots of math. I guess you get that from your father." She closed the report. "Well, thank you very much. That's—interesting. I'll look at it more later."

She reached behind her, dropped my thesis on top of the newspaper pile, and laughed sharply. "Well, of course I know a few things about unemployment myself."

Her sarcasm was unmistakable, and the sting of rejection had not fully registered before I was suffused with fury. I had the impression that for much of her first decade in California she hadn't worked at all, and had only found a job when the welfare office forced her to. With difficulty I managed to bite back my own retort—*No, you don't. You wouldn't even show up in those numbers, because to be counted as unemployed you had to be looking for work, and that wasn't happening, was it?*

I tried again. "This is a pretty neighborhood. What are those pink flowers around the door? Did you plant them?"

I knew she used to like gardening. We never had grass at the Ypsilanti house, but Mama helped me plant moss roses and bachelor buttons in a quarter-round plot at the corner of the yard. She said I could choose what to grow, but I knew she loved the ragged blue cornflowers and silky pink-and-orange Portulaca, so those were the seeds I picked out. (She never got around to making a garden in Ann Arbor, maybe because she was writing more by then.)

"Oh, no, that's just bougainvillea, that stuff grows everywhere." She leaned forward in the butterfly chair to peer through the front window, then gestured toward the rear door. "I'm going to plant a garden out back, but first I have to get a compost pile going and convince our neighbor it won't draw flies. I explained to him that it won't. Everybody knows that once you get it balanced right and it heats up it doesn't smell at all. It takes care of itself." She settled more deeply in the canvas sling, with a complacent smile. "But you know, he can't see past the nose on his face, like most people."

Silence. Marina shifted from one foot to another. "How was your flight?" she asked suddenly. I said the trip from D.C. was awfully long, but smooth, and that I'd liked flying down the coast from San Francisco to L.A., seeing the beaches and pretty islands. Then Mama said she didn't understand why anyone would want to fly when it was so obviously dangerous and ridiculously expensive. She thought everybody should take the train, or better yet the bus—if they really had to travel in the first place, like some people seemed to think they should.

Yes, I know that's what you think. And how was I supposed to get all the way out here to see you? I didn't, of course, actually say that; I was not sure, now, that I had anything left to say to her. I'd imagined that all I had to do was overlook her eccentric attitudes and lifestyle, forgive her for leaving, and find the courage to face the mother I'd never known as an adult. I'd come to regret the antipathy I had first copied from my father and then adopted as my own, and was ready to be more open and accepting, but I had it all backward. She'd run away, I was trying to find her, but she didn't want to be found and didn't care if I liked her or not. What was starting to become clear was that she didn't like me much at all.

THE PLEASURE OF YOUR COMPANY
(WASHINGTON, 1988)

"Was it Northeast or Southeast?" My mother and I both remembered that Nanny's house had been at Eighth and A, but Capitol Hill is where the four quadrants of the city come together; there is an A Street one block north of East Capitol and another A Street a block south. We knew the house had been near Lincoln Park, but that grassy rectangle lies exactly on the east-west axis and didn't settle the question. At 8th and A Northeast, a red brick townhouse was, we agreed, close, but not quite right, and I drove around the block and headed south.

"That's it!" She recognized the house, and once I pulled to the curb in front of 27 Eighth Street, SE, it felt like I did, too. What surprised me is that, rather than seeming smaller than it had to my four-year-old eyes, the two-story Victorian, with its imposing corner tower, was huge. The trolley tracks were gone, the entire block much-gentrified, but the wrought-iron fence still stood. I noted the corner windows and their curved glass panes. We sat in the car and gazed across the street.

"Is that the window?" I pointed to the double-hung sash on the second floor.

"It must be." My mother nodded slowly. "I wasn't really there, though. I was in the bathtub or something, hungover, or maybe just depressed. I don't know where your father was. I didn't know about it until it was all over." She recounted this calmly, in a bemused tone that seemed to suggest it didn't matter much what had happened and who had been there. I didn't say anything about an already-broken arm or the statute of limitations.

My third husband and I didn't actually meet in a grief support group, as touching as that might have been. It had taken me probably a year too long to accept the fact that I belonged to a club I'd never wanted to join, to meet other young widows struggling along that unfamiliar and stony path, and to begin to consider what I might make of the rest of my life.

After a year had passed since my second husband's first-and-final heart attack, I'd gone on a few dates, but hadn't met anyone I really connected with. Two nice men clearly hoped that, fully recovered from an unfortunate experience, I would become once again the woman I'd been *before*, put my three-year marriage and its shocking end behind me, and move on. I didn't know what I was going to do, but I knew "getting back to normal" wasn't possible. My new friends and I agreed about that. I was thinking of changing my life a lot—leaving my policy analyst job, taking the hated life insurance money and using it to go back to school. I might become a psychologist.

THE GOOD POETIC MOTHER

"You should talk to"—I don't know, now, how my fellow support-group member (even younger than I) knew the man I would marry the following year. She told me he'd been an up-and-coming government lawyer before his wife got sick. Since losing her, he'd left all that behind, started up an independent practice, and was trying to be of help, one-on-one, to other people whose lives weren't turning out the way they expected.

I met him at the beginning of February, and we were engaged in March. We bought a house in July, and by October we were married and I was pregnant. Despite its headlong beginning, it has turned out to be a long marriage, and from the first it seemed to give me a secure enough base to pick up some of the parts of my life I'd set aside. We visited California in the summer of 1987 for a reunion of my husband's family, then added on, seven years after my first disappointing effort to find my mother, a trip to Ocean Park to see her. Her own mother was still alive, and while I have only a fuzzy recollection of the visit, I do have a photograph that my husband took at the nursing home not far from my mother's apartment. Briefly, and against all odds, there were four generations together—Grandma Dean, Mama, me, and my baby daughter.

I knew by now that trying to forget painful events and difficult people was not a sustainable strategy. As I had in 1981, I felt it would be worth trying to have some relationship, no matter how limited, with my mother, and I decided to invite her to visit us in Washington the next summer. She had enjoyed talking to my husband (throughout her life she got on better with men than with women) and accepted both the invitation and the train ticket. I hoped the visit would give me a chance to talk to her openly, to tell her of the things I'd gone through in the decades when we were apart, perhaps get to know her better.

THE PLEASURE OF YOUR COMPANY (WASHINGTON, 1988)

It wasn't easy. She wanted to be known—she sang "Joe Hill" for my toddler, demanded to know why the neighborhood bookstore, Politics and Prose, didn't include *poetry* as part of their name, and asked the clerk if they had anything by Charles Bukowski (and if not, why not)—but didn't have much interest in me. She seemed determined at times to be a caricature of a loopy California hippie; when I confided my obsessive, post-traumatic fears that something terrible would happen to my third husband; she told me of a friend who warded off heart disease by listening to "lots of reggae music."

I hoped she'd like the American City Diner, a retro malt shop just a few blocks from my house, and she did laugh at the posters—*Eat and Get Out,* and *No Whining Allowed.* "So what's good here?" she asked.

I knew what I liked (the hamburger) but couldn't imagine what she might want.

"Oh, a fried egg sandwich! That's perfect." She told me she used to make fried egg sandwiches for us back in Michigan, in the house on South Grove Road where she had only a two-burner hot plate and no stove. I wished I could remember that. I wished I could remember anything good about that house.

But the burger was perfect, the French fries still hot, and my mother's visit was almost over. I was feeling, for the moment, more or less at ease with her. She hadn't asked me about graduate school, except to comment, "I'm glad you're doing what you want, finally." That might have been the most important thing about my endeavor, but I was deep in the literature review for my dissertation, and wanted to tell her about the thoughts I was developing. My topic was trauma and bereavement (of course), and she had made no comment on that inevitable choice. I explained the limitations of psychology's "medical model," how that way of thinking regards loss or injury as akin to illness, grief and despair as symptoms, and recovery as a return to baseline. I knew, and was sure she'd agree, that there are some experiences that change you forever, after which there may be healing, but no going back to being the person you once had been. I was interested in how catastrophe can be a catalyst for change, growth, and, sometimes, a more meaningful life. It was all pretty high-minded and idealistic, but I was excited, and failed to realize that she was not particularly enjoying hearing me go on about my own life and projects.

Finally, I noticed her smirk. "Oh, really?" She turned away, hoisted her coffee mug to signal the waitress for a refill. "Changed forever, you think? Yes, well, that's a popular idea, I suppose."

I didn't try to tell her anything more. I was stung, but I didn't need her approval, or my father's, or anyone else's, to know what was important to me and what I wanted to do. I had been changed.

Her train was due to leave Union Station at four, and we had another hour before heading downtown. She was sitting at the kitchen island, finishing the tuna salad sandwich I made for her. I like tuna, but now the fishy smell put me off. I wasn't hungry, and I had something I needed to say.

"So, how has this visit been for you?" I began.

She was gazing out the window, at the crimson roses in full July bloom against the garage. "How has it been? Being here? Oh, fine! It's been just great."

I'd imagined she, too, had been thinking how momentous those two weeks had been—together now, almost three decades after she

THE PLEASURE OF YOUR COMPANY (WASHINGTON, 1988)

left, talking for the first time about the life she and my father and my sisters and I once led.

I turned away, filled the copper kettle and set it carefully on the stove. "We have time for a cup of tea, if you'd like." I kept my voice neutral, neither angry nor particularly warm.

"Oh, that would be nice. You're sure there's enough time?" I filled a china teapot with boiling water, dumped it out after a minute, and added two scoops of black tea and the remaining water. I covered the pot in a tea cozy I'd made a few years back when I started to learn what a "proper" teatime could be, and assembled the tray as if laying out sacred objects for a religious ceremony—matching sugar bowl, milk jug, cups and saucers. I had bought the flowered, gold-trimmed bone china after my husband died, when my despair had brought on fears of descending into the kind of chaotic and squalid life I'd had with my mother. I'd needed to surround myself with comfort and beauty as a kind of charm to keep myself safe. And alive.

The past two weeks with my mother had triggered unwanted feelings and memories that occupied my waking mind and my dreams, colliding with my mother's infuriatingly neutral commentary on the years we had shared. I was angry at who she still was, at being reminded so forcefully of who she had been when she *was* my mother, and of how radically insecure our connection had always been. Before her visit I'd imagined myself more than ready to forgive her, and perhaps even believed I already had. But I had not fully realized the extent to which forgiveness is transactional. It works best, of course, if one party *asks* the other's forgiveness, and is able to hear of the aggrieved party's suffering, but it was clear now that my mother was not going to ask to hear my story (let alone ask for my forgiveness). As her visit was coming to an end, I remained afraid to confront her. Maybe I didn't want to cause her pain, or perhaps I didn't want to see myself as an avenger. I had been hoping to transcend the gritty facts of my past, but it was clear now that I had not achieved that elevated perspective.

I'd been feeling more each day that I was punishing *myself* by not speaking the truth to her. Wasn't I doing the same thing with her that I had for so long done with my father—as if it were agreed between us that, *yes you mistreated me and you hurt me and the hurt has been part of my whole life, but we will never speak of any of it. I'm still alive, so it's all right.* Wasn't I saying again, by my silence, that it had been fine, because they couldn't have done better and probably I wasn't worth better.

"Well, I'm afraid this has all been pretty tough for me." I poured the tea. "I've been thinking so much about things I guess I try not to remember—what it was like when you and Daddy were together and fighting so much, and then that last year in Ann Arbor with you, and especially what my life was like after you left us with Daddy." She raised one eyebrow, but said nothing.

"I have to tell you, it was just—it wasn't okay."

She hadn't been expecting that, and quickly, she was angry. "Oh, it wasn't, wasn't it? Not okay?" She took her cup and saucer to the sink, lips pressed tightly together, and walked out of the kitchen.

We didn't continue that conversation. Although I know I must have put her bag in the car, driven across Rock Creek Park to South Capitol Street and down to Massachusetts Avenue, and dropped her off at the high-arched main entrance of Union Station, I don't remember saying goodbye.

We survived that visit, and it was a turning point that gave us a chance to pick up where we'd left off in 1981. Like that first meeting, this had been an awkward and upsetting encounter in many ways, but afterwards we were able to sustain a connection that would last the rest of her life. I could see the limits that would always be placed on our relationship, but we had carved out a space that, while cramped, allowed us to know one another.

She wrote a thank-you note while still on the train. (Despite her cultivated unconventionality, she was good at what she called "bread-and-butter letters.") She had spent a day in Chicago, and had found "a really lively poetry scene there, as you may have heard." (I hadn't heard of Chicago's poetry scene; it would be many years before I would come to appreciate writing and its scenes.)

The end of her note was more personal. "Words cannot express my thanks to you for this wonderful vacation. It was extremely generous of you to take such good care of me. And thank you for telling me off. It was painful, but it was necessary."

She'd been wrong to be angry at me, she wrote, and admitted she had been jealous of my comfortable house and apparently easy life. Just as when I visited her in California the first time, my survival looked like "success" to her, making me the kind of person whose accomplishments threatened to make her feel inferior, and rather than hate herself, she had hated me.

There were more visits, more letters, somewhat more honesty and certainly more kindness after that. In her late seventies she commented on her short-term memory (not so good) and her long-term memory (better), writing that she could remember clearly "the trip that you financed in 1988. I often think about what a great mother you are and credit you with inventing yourself as a mother, as I know I was not a good mother to you."

NOTHING TO SAY (WASHINGTON, 1984, 1994, 2000, 2004)

I sat next to my ten-year-old son in the front pew at the Arlington Unitarian Church, perspiring in a black rayon dress. The minister was the one I'd known as a child in Michigan, who had moved to D.C. around the time my father did, and who had officiated at my wedding three years and two months earlier. I heard only some of what he said, and hoped I'd given him enough guidance so that his words might be ones my just-departed husband would have appreciated. I was satisfied with my choice of music, though I wouldn't be able to remember later what it was. Bach, probably.

My mother was not at the service. Nor, for that matter, were any of my sisters. Survivors of a family that had been not so much broken as atomized, we were by now scattered too far, and had each suffered too much, to help one another. All happy families may be, as Tolstoy claimed, alike, staying in touch and gathering for weddings and for funerals, but unhappy families are sometimes too fractured to either grieve or celebrate together.

NOTHING TO SAY (WASHINGTON, 1984, 1994, 2000, 2004)

In the early 1900s, neither set of my grandparents had any family present when they married. Twenty years later, my own parents were married by a justice of the peace, with a borrowed stranger as their witness. My mother did not attend any of my three weddings, and of my sisters' various marriages (seven in all) I was present at only two.

Ten years after that Arlington funeral, finished with graduate school and teaching part-time, I was working in my study when my husband (that unexpected third husband) called up the stairs, telling me to turn the radio on. "Your mother's on NPR!"

Charles Bukowski, diagnosed with leukemia just a few months earlier, had died on the ninth of March, 1994. Scott Simon introduced "the L.A. poet francEyE, who lived with Bukowski in the early 1960s and is the mother of his only child." She told the reporter that Bukowski "saw his writing as what he was supposed to be doing in the world." She had admired the "discipline that he had about it—writing every day," as if in response to a "harsh punishing voice that drives you to do something, whether you want to or not." He had often said, she recalled, "this typewriter is my father."

I recognized by then my mother's writing name; she had written to me in the late 1980s, enclosing some poems, and in a postscript added, "I signed the poems francEyE, then realized you maybe had never heard this name, which I use all the time now. It was given me by a friend at work."

I knew that I should write to Marina. My half-sister had a real father, not a typewriter—in fact a more loving father than mine—and now had lost him. Somehow I didn't get around to it. Something that would have let me be that generous person was either never in me to start with, or else (and this is what it felt like) had been killed off when my mother left. In the days that followed I felt inexplicably sad; I told a friend that I supposed there had been a death in the family.

My mother published her first collection of poems, *Snaggletooth in Ocean Park*, two years later. The title refers to the poem Bukowski wrote about her, "One for Old Snaggletooth." When I called to congratulate her, she said that she had come to believe that Bukowski had to die before she could fully put herself forward as a poet.

When my own father died, a few months into the new century, it was my mother who telephoned from California to tell me of the death of her ex-husband, an event that had occurred barely two miles away from where I lived. We were both surprised at how undone I was by the news. I had not been in contact with my father for fifteen years, ever since my post-widowhood emotional breakdown had made clear how impossible it was to maintain a relationship with him while trying to ignore our shared history. Now I wasn't at all sure what to do about his funeral.

My mother had been married to him for seventeen years. She wrote a poem on the day he died, and I don't know if she noticed the fact (I only realized this after she was gone, too) that the eponymous date was also the anniversary of their wedding, more than a half-century before.

> *MAY 19*
> *He's dead. There's nothing to say*
> *. . . .*

NOTHING TO SAY (WASHINGTON, 1984, 1994, 2000, 2004)

My clock broke the day he died.
Time's gone away at last.
....
He's dead. There's nothing to say.
I've been begging myself to die,
and he was the one who heard,
but he never knew who I am.
....
I'm alive, with nothing to say.

francEyE, May 2000

She sent me the poem, along with a more considered reflection on who my father had been. She'd felt some relief when she finished this poem, but at the same time thought she might have been too harsh. My father had "some wonderful qualities," she wrote. "He was there in a pinch; when he knew what to do, he did it. He couldn't stand not knowing what to do, and would hurt other people, whoever they were, when he was scared or hurt."

His death, she reflected, had given her a particular kind of release. "When someone dies, part of us dies. I think the part of me that wanted to die so often is the part that's died now. That's the part that sees myself as an incompetent bungler and gets really tired of feeling that way. That's not just me in relation to your father, it's me in relation to my mom to begin with, but it didn't die when she did."

I recognized here the consequence of living with someone who banished his own self-doubt by projecting all inadequacy onto others—his wife and daughters in particular. Over time his relentless contempt was inevitably absorbed by his targets. We all struggled not to regard ourselves as inherently inferior—stupid, lazy, inept—as my father had, in order to rationalize his mistreatment, convinced himself we were. I understood very well how that experience over enough years might eventually make a person want to die, and thought that my mother's escape to California may have been as much as anything a flight for her life.

Her experience of Bukowski's death had been quite different. He had not needed to make her feel inadequate, and that chronically suicidal part of her, she wrote, "wasn't important in my relation to Hank, not so much because of me as because of him." Although they hadn't been able to go on living together, she had always respected and admired him. After Bukowski died she had begun to realize that "I had to construct for myself the power I had that I gave to him."

I didn't have to wonder long what to do about my father's funeral—Sara telephoned within hours, relaying the message that our stepmother wanted me to come, that she needed me. I was confused, surprised, and relieved, and the next day I found myself sitting with my sisters Sara and Ruthie, our stepmother, and our half-sister Anne, considering the merits of various astronomically-priced funeral packages. The viewing was at Gawler's funeral home, and I recognized the room where Nanny had been "laid out" in 1967. As we waited in line to pass by our father's casket, I asked Sara if she remembered Nanny saying, when she'd been waiting too long for someone, "I had you laid out in seven shades of purple." We were glad to have something to smile about, a small memory to share.

My father looked like himself, not much changed since the last time I'd seen him, fifteen years earlier. Except, of course, that he was dead. I tried to feel something like love, and managed to acknowledge, perhaps to both of us, *you were my father*. All week, Sara and Ruthie and I had been ending almost every conversation about him with some version of "he did the best he could."

NOTHING TO SAY (WASHINGTON, 1984, 1994, 2000, 2004)

It was my father's death that began a transformation in how my sisters and I related to each other. Four of his five daughters—including his youngest, but not the oldest—attended his funeral, and that ritual seemed to lift a spell that had separated me from my sisters even longer than I'd been cut off from him. It wasn't only that the awkwardness of having placed myself outside the family was dissolved, but something more fundamental. Not only were we not competing for his imagined approval, we were no longer afraid of him.

My own absence had freed me from the subtle but constant rivalry and "taking sides" that had so long pitted the sisters against one another. When I still knew my father, I had sided with him in tacit rejection of my mother and my runaway older sister. I regret to recall that I held my two younger sisters in a kind of limbo, as possibly not people I wanted to know. His death gave me a chance to do better, to reunite with those sisters, to see them clearly and without comparison or judgment.

Ruthie, the youngest, ran away to an ashram when she was a teenager, changed her name to Gurunam, left the ashram, married, became Prashad, divorced, and changed her name to Skye. She now had a teenaged son, and they came from California for our father's funeral. I had been sure I wouldn't recognize her, but when she walked through the arrival gate at Baltimore-Washington International Airport, it was like looking into a mirror.

Sara, the second-youngest, had lived not very far from me for years, but we'd seen little of each other. Her first marriage and a second one had ended, and she'd fled another relationship when she thought her children were at risk. By the time our father died, she (like our mother) had given up on men, and her life was more stable. By that time, too, I had given up trying to feel superior to other people, and was trying to be a better person myself.

THE GOOD POETIC MOTHER

I had so long removed myself from the rest of the family—a self-protective stance no longer necessary—that it was startling to be part of it again. Finally, my sisters and I could compare notes about the life we'd shared and had hardly ever talked about, a precious opportunity even if the validation and fascination of these exchanges came at the cost of recurrent bleak moods and bad dreams.

"Well, the story I got—" This was the recurrent qualifier in the talks Sara, Ruthie and I were finally having. "Do we even know for sure why he got custody?" I asked the other two. The three of us were in my kitchen the day after burying our father, drinking too much coffee, and amazed to be together. Sara thought it might have been about money. "It cost him more when we lived with her. Didn't he have to pay child support?" I hadn't considered that particular piece of the familiar puzzle.

We had trouble piecing together how events played out at the very end. We'd been in the Morningside Drive house with Mama, then she was suddenly gone. "But how did we get to D.C.?" I wanted to know. Sara remembered spending the first motherless (and sleepless) night with the next-door neighbors, then riding in a car with Mrs. Cohen. While Ruthie didn't disagree, neither she nor I could say how we ourselves had gotten from our mother and Ann Arbor to our father and Washington.

Ruthie wanted to go back further, asking, "Where did we live when I was born?" She, of course, had the fewest memories of all of us, and Sara and I tried to fill in some of the family history. We'd been in Michigan for almost three years, and were living in the house on South Grove Road when Ruthie came along. Sara remembered that house a little. "We never had a lawn like other people in the neighborhood."

But then she wondered, "Why were we in Michigan in the first place?"

"Well, the story I got—" I began. They cracked up.

We each tried to say what our earliest memories were. Mine, of course, was about Patti going out the window, when we lived with Nanny and Patti and I were four and two. The story I'd gotten about that, the playing tag and running too fast, didn't really hang together. Sara and Ruthie had both had some contact with Patti over the years, and had also heard what she believed about that morning in Nanny's house. "He pushed her, she thinks. Could it be he *threw* her out the window?" Sara speculated. We couldn't rule anything out.

We talked about our father, acknowledging his strengths as well as his failings. We shared how terrible he had made each of us feel about ourselves, and those conversations began to heal some of the damage. We agreed that underneath his facade of superiority he had been insecure, and needed to make other people feel weak and defective to prop up his own self-image. (I think this is what my mother meant about how her relationship with Bukowski had been different. Whatever his faults, the Great Poet had never been a bully.)

We talked, of course, about our mother. Sara and Ruthie knew her better than I did—in the years when I had so resolutely kept my distance, they had been more curious about her, and perhaps less afraid. After her early wanderings, Ruthie had landed in Southern California herself, and over the years Sara had taken her own daughters to meet their poet grandmother. Now we could turn over, together, the impossible conundrums of *why did she leave, of course she had to leave, was it okay, how could it be okay.*

I said I had long assumed that it had been because she was a creative person, always needed to be a free spirit, and that taking care of four children was more than she could manage. Ruthie wondered, though, "But what about—"

And Sara finished her thought—"Marina?" Our mother's daughter with Bukowski was thirty-five, as hard as that was for me to fathom. How did we feel about her? Sara smiled wryly. "I can never figure out if I ought to be mad at Marina because she got to grow up with our mother, or if I should feel sorry for her—"

Ruthie and I joined in, "Because she got to grow up with our mother!"

We told stories about Mama—walking an equal-housing picket line with her on a snowy day in Michigan, her autoharp and *The Fireside Book of Folk Songs*, the "Multipurpose Food" she thought we could all live on when she ran out of child support money, how she stayed up all night writing poems and letters to the editor.

The three of us were connected again, even if Patti remained in her own world. And when Ruthie died, four years after our father (in her sleep, in her forties, of undiagnosed heart damage), Sara and I and our mother had a chance to lay her to rest and grieve together.

Ruthie had lived in California for most of her adult life, and at the time of her death was living not far from our mother. They knew many of the same people and Ruthie sometimes attended the Church in Ocean Park, the activist congregation our mother had joined decades earlier. We held her memorial service there. I was in a daze the whole weekend, unable to speak about my baby sister in front of all those strangers. I'd known her as a small child, when she was probably the most neglected of the four of us, but almost not at all after she left home so young. We had just been beginning to figure out, in the few years since our father's death, who we were to one another.

At the end of the service, the participants were invited to walk together to the beach, for a "farewell at the shore," bringing floral arrangements from the church and throwing them into the water. I met people who had known my mother all the time that I had not, and discovered that while certainly very liberal, even radical, in their political and social views, they were mostly sane. Many of them held my mother in high esteem, if sometimes in a slightly intimidated way, and after returning home I received a mailing that illustrated that fact. A gala was to be held at our mother's church, to celebrate the "Sixth annual Communitas Awards, honoring local community members ...including local poet francEyE." There would be dinner, then the awards and musical entertainment, and a donation of fifty dollars was requested. This invitation to celebrate my mother, to *admire* her, was not one I was quite ready to accept; I still couldn't reconcile that attitude with how I'd felt about her for so many years. I did not make a donation, but neither did I try to erase her from my life again.

My mother was deeply affected by this latest loss, and a few months later wrote this poem:

> *COUNTING*
> *When I was 35, my husband said*
> *"Well, Fran, you're half-way there."*
> *What could he have meant? But though*
> *we didn't subscribe to the bible*
> *what he meant was*
> *3 score and 10 are the years we expect.*
> *He lived 6 extra and I've lived 12 so far*
> *so we owe this daughter*
> *dead at 46*
> *(or I owe her*
> *since he can no longer pay)*

6.
I owe her 6.
I may die still in debt. She wants me
to go on. I'll try,
but living this way, living with her gone,
is not quite living. I can grieve, though, grieve,
for as long as she wants.

francEyE, 2004

GRANDMA STORIES (CALIFORNIA, 2007)

"Join Us For An Eighty-fifth Birthday Poetry Fest and Fundraiser!" read the email's subject line. Dated March 14, 2007, it was from a Los Angeles literary organization called CobaltPoets, and the writer whose birthday would be celebrated was my mother.

"Longtime Los Angeles poet francEyE has one birthday wish this year: to publish her *Grandma Stories* book of poems. So we're having a fundraising party to help make her wish come true." The event would be at the end of the month, and for a reasonable admission—"$5 to $20, sliding scale"—patrons would hear francEyE read a few poems and enjoy wine, cheese, music and good company.

Well, that sounded very nice. This must be the book my mother had mentioned off and on for the last year or so, a collection of prose poems that would comprise, she hoped, a memoir. She'd sent me some of the individual pieces, but I hadn't realized the project was finished.

I went back through emails from my mother—she wrote a lot, and I didn't always read her poems immediately. I came across one, unread, that was headed, "Here It Is!" The email included what I now realized *was* the entire set of poems. It was time to read the story of my mother's life.

I printed out the forty-plus pages and settled in a comfortable chair, my feet on an ottoman. The book was dedicated to "Grandson #4," and I imagined that my half-sister's son, born after Bukowski's death, was the friendly audience that my mother needed to hold in mind when tackling difficult material. She had ten other grandchildren (including my own son and daughter), but, being fond of the sweet ten-year-old who bore Bukowski's name, I told myself I was okay with that choice.

The narrator in each prose poem was "Grandma," at various ages. There were accounts of "Baby Grandma" in Maine, and of "First-Grade Grandma" in Brooklyn. When her father fell ill, "Second-Grade Grandma" took the train with her mother to the hospital at Saranac Lake but could only see her father through a high window. "Third-Grade Grandma" refused to believe it when she was told he had died.

Life had been a bit happier for "Teen Grandma," and "Soldier Grandma" had adventures I'd never heard about. I kept myself from skipping ahead, although I was eager to find the poems that would be about me and my sisters, maybe even our father.

The final poem began, "Poet Grandma was lonesome, so she wrote a letter to the world's greatest poet and told him she would like to meet him."

A headache that had been slowly gathering for the past quarter-hour now began to pound in earnest. I checked the pages—maybe I'd skipped over something—but there was nothing between the next-to-last piece—"*Rank/1944*"—and the final one "*New Life/1963.*" Two decades, including the seventeen years when she and my father were married, when she had been my mother, were omitted from this memoir. It was as if neither I nor my three sisters had ever existed, or perhaps had been willfully erased. I stood up abruptly, the sheaf of papers sliding to the floor. I was not in my mother's book, and I was not okay with that.

Once I thought I had my voice under control, I telephoned Sara.

"Am I missing something here?" I asked. Sara had also received the invitation, and had her own set of our mother's poems, but our copies were identical; there were not, as I somehow continued to hope, any additional poems. Neither of us were inclined to respond to the fundraiser invitation.

After the shock subsided, however, I began to consider that there might be another reason to visit California. I'd always hoped my mother would someday be ready to volunteer more information about our life together and how it had ended, and had been reluctant to ask her about things she didn't want to discuss. Now, it seemed increasingly likely that she wasn't going to tell us more if we didn't ask her directly.

Our half-sister's wedding gave us a reason to fly to San Francisco in December. Our mother was staying with Marina before returning to her own apartment in Ocean Park, and on the morning after the warm and moving ceremony, Sara and I drove over to the stucco bungalow on a quiet street near Berkeley. Mama was wearing a flowered tunic over a once-white thermal undershirt and faded black cotton pants. The long braid was gone, her thinning white hair cut short, but the unplucked hairs on her chin that had earned her the nickname in Southern California poetry circles of "The Bearded Witch of Ocean Park," remained. She had an inhaler on a string around her neck, and a detailed schedule for her medications. A visiting nurse would be looking in later in the day.

"If you don't mind," I said politely, "I'd like to record this." I was cheerful, friendly, only somewhat duplicitous, suggesting that francEyE's other grandchildren would certainly be interested in hearing more about her.

"We wanted to ask you"—I stopped, swallowed hard, and began again. "We hoped we could talk about the time that you were with Daddy—you know, the part of your life that's not in the *Grandma Stories*? Would that be okay?" I was grateful for Sara's presence, but I was six years older, I was the one who had brought the recorder, and I would have to get the ball rolling.

As she would repeat several times over the next two hours, our mother said she couldn't remember. She tried to make a joke of it, smiling weakly. "Well, I don't—let me think now, when was that? Who is Daddy?"

Sara and I chuckled politely.

Our questions started at the beginning. How did our parents meet? (We did not ask what in the world made them think getting married was a good idea.) I was hoping to somehow work up to my real questions—*after all those years of fighting, what finally blew up their marriage? Why did she leave? How did we all end up with our father?*

"I met him in the Army, shortly before the war ended, in the spring. I was on a Signal Corps post on the campus of a former girls' school, Arlington Hall." Once she got going about the war and the WACs, her voice was stronger, and she leaned toward us slightly.

"He was on a post up the road that was all men, and they used to come down whenever they could and hang out. I would go over to the rec hall and play records on my day off and they would come over and sit and see the women."

The work was top secret, "all devoted to decoding messages, it was some system that has been written about since, but you did just your part and you didn't know what it was all about." Thinking back, I realized that neither of our parents had ever told us anything about what they actually did in the war. If they couldn't even talk to one another about how they spent their days, what drew them together?

"Oh, God knows. He kind of scared me." The logic of that eluded me, but Mama went on to tell how, when her grandmother died and she was granted an emergency leave to go to California for the funeral, our father "wanted me to go see his folks in Pasadena when I was here, so I did." Recalling how forceful he could be, how one's own aims and ideas would evaporate in the face of his indomitable will, I found this entirely plausible.

"He met me when I flew back—I took military flights almost all the way, and a commercial plane the last route. And in years afterwards I would remember that moment when I met him at the airport. He's standing there, glaring and fuming, WHERE *WERE* YOU?" Mama shouted these last words, and Sara and I flinched, remembering our father's voice. "I should have been warned then, and never gotten married to him."

She recalled the earliest days of the marriage. "I'd say, why are you talking to me like that? You never used to talk to me like that! And he'd say well, I guess it's because you're part of me now."

We all recalled his impatience, his need to blame someone if he was upset or worried, how he could turn nasty without warning.

"Do you remember asking me where is the middle of next week?" Mama asked me.

Sara interjected, "Because he was going to throw you into the middle of next week?"

I tried to back up a bit. Where did they get married? And when?

THE GOOD POETIC MOTHER

"Oh, in D.C., we went and found somebody who was open on a Sunday. We got married the day I got back." Sara and I exchanged a glance expressing shock, incredulity, and perhaps recognition.

I asked if the two of them had ever "thought about how many kids you were going to have." Had they expected to have four children?

Our mother grimaced and shook her head ruefully. "No, it was so stupid. How are you going to get out of the Army? Well, I could get pregnant. Just assuming that's what you did in life, not having the faintest idea what it was all about."

Mama reflected on the ensuing years, and I added the little I could remember. My older sister and I had been born in D.C., where our parents finished college on the GI Bill. We moved to California, and they separated twice in three years. Reconciled again, they moved to Michigan and had another baby. Those first years in Ypsilanti were not easy, with a fourth baby soon after the third, our father often rageful and frightening, and our mother repeatedly too depressed to get out of bed.

She recalled recurring obsessive fears "of driving over somebody, of killing a child. Every time we'd go over a bump that fear would come up again. And really what I was telling myself is that there was something I was living that was not healthy for my children."

After five years in Ypsilanti, we had moved to Ann Arbor. Remembering that moving-up-in-the-world transition, our discussion became more animated, as we each recalled details of the new house at the crest of Morningside Drive—the open plan, modern linoleum floor, cathedral ceilings, and tall windows. I remembered a party, asked if she had really made angel food cake with strawberries and sour cream. Mama nodded in recognition, then filled in more of that long-ago menu. "I read in a women's magazine about fondue, so I got the pot and the ingredients and served fondue."

Tentatively, I asked if she and my father had been "more or less happy at that time?" She did not contradict me. "Well, yes, in a way we were. Because I was making friends and had a place to express myself, and he was doing well in his job, moving ahead." That fit my own recollection of the brief years that had always seemed to me the sanest and best time of my childhood.

"But then Daddy got the job in Washington, right?" I asked. I remembered that Wilbur Cohen, a colleague from the University of Michigan, had joined the Kennedy Administration and found my father a job on Capitol Hill where he would be useful to the New Frontier. It was going to make life even better for all of us, I'd thought.

Mama recalled the winter and spring of 1961, when our father lived in D.C., returning to Ann Arbor every few weeks. At the end of the school year the whole family was going to move to Washington. I'd always believed that was what ended the marriage, imagining that if we'd never left Michigan, my parents might have stayed together, but Mama didn't agree.

"I don't think we would have stayed together very much longer anyway." Sometime during those months when our father was away in Washington, she'd heard an expert speak at the Unitarian church about juvenile delinquency. "And the root cause, he found, was a fundamental disagreement about basic things between the parents. I listened to this and kind of did an internal spin."

Sara offered, "So suddenly staying together for the children was not the right thing to do?" and our mother nodded emphatically. "Exactly."

At this point I fell back on my repeated prompt. "So, then what happened?"

She frowned and stared past us. "Well, now my mind is kind of a blank. I remember one time he was back on the weekend, we'd had a party, the party was over, we went outside." Inevitably, they had begun to fight.

"We were arguing, and he said, 'I can't take it anymore.' And I said, 'Well OK, we'll quit then.' And he said, 'What do you mean?' And I said, 'Well, you can't take it, so leave, or get a divorce.' And he was shocked."

That was a fight I've always recalled, at the beginning of a crazy weekend when they shouted, made up, fought more—and then our father took my sisters and me with him to Washington, leaving our mother behind.

"So then I got a divorce. You know there was no such thing as women's rights yet, but there were paternalistic lawyers." Our father hadn't wanted the divorce, "and at one point my lawyer and your father's lawyer had me come into the office for a talk, and they told me that they thought that I might need psychiatric counseling, and asked me if I was willing to have a consultation with a psychiatrist."

I gasped aloud at this point, but she went on.

"I said sure! And I went and I had this hour-long consultation with a psychiatrist of their choice, and he decided that I did not need psychiatric counseling. Which was very disappointing to your father and his lawyer."

My sisters and I had been with our father in Washington for six months, only rarely seeing our mother and becoming increasingly miserable. Mama said to me, "You and Patti didn't like school, and you in particular were really scared in school, so he asked me to take the kids, all of them, back to Ann Arbor."

Patti had been fifteen, I was thirteen, and the little girls were six and four when we returned with our mother to Morningside Drive.

I rejoined my class in the middle of eighth grade, hoping that life would be at least more peaceful without our father.

That arrangement lasted not quite a year.

"I wasn't very good at it," Mama said. "Well, of course he didn't give me much to live on." Those were the increasingly chaotic months I'd once tried so hard to forget. Again I prompted, "Then what happened?"

Perhaps she didn't want to go any farther down that darkening road. "It's hard to remember."

She looked tired, and I tried to help her out.

"Well, one thing that happened is that Patti started running away," I offered.

She agreed, "Patti ran away to be a singer, in Detroit."

Sara remembered hearing Patti perform, going along when Mama "went up to check on Patti." Mama sometimes spent the night at the coffeehouse where Patti sang (a venue called, as I suddenly remembered, "The UnStabled"), while my little sisters and I stayed with various neighbors and friends in Ann Arbor.

The almost-final debacle came when Patti was picked up by the police "with a bunch of other kids, for smoking dope," and our mother had gone to the police station to try to bail her out. "The policewoman didn't like me, and I didn't like her, and she arrested me for contributing to the delinquency of a minor."

Sara and I were literally openmouthed at this point, but our mother was animated, recalling what seemed to have morphed from tragedy to comedy after four-and-a-half decades. She had called her divorce lawyer, who "came and got us and promised that we would never come back to Detroit again."

This was sounding like an action movie, an engaging adventure about two feisty girls on the lam.

"Of course, Patti did go right back to Detroit," Mama concluded.

"I guess the question is"—I was finding it a little hard to breathe—"how did Daddy get all of us?"

Her primary concern back then had been trying to keep Patti out of trouble. "I said to your father, 'Will you take the young ones for a while so I can deal with Patti,' and he said, 'Well, if you sign this.'"

For a while. She hadn't intended it to be permanent?

She went on, "You know it seems strange to me that I didn't say, well, what do you mean *sign this*? I didn't have a sense of—what? Negotiation."

She had signed away custody without actually reading the document. I closed my eyes for a moment, then tried to say something that might soften that awful truth. "I imagine you were very worried about Patti."

"Oh, I was," she replied. "I had miserable nightmares about her, I would see her running in the forest and looking so scared, and I would try and find her, and she'd be running, so scared, all night long."

Sara frowned, trying to put all this in the context of her own seven-year-old memories. She remembered our mother "giving me the choice of whether I wanted to stay with you or whether I wanted to go to Daddy, but I don't think there was really any choice." She shook her head, sadly. "I remember telling you that I wanted to go visit with him for a while."

With her three younger daughters in D.C. again, Mama went back to Detroit, trying to live with Patti, who still wouldn't stay with her. Finally, she gave up. "I just said, 'I'm going to have to let her go. I can't help her. I don't know what to do.' So I wrote to her and said I didn't want her to come to me anymore."

At this point, for the first time in the long conversation, she looked as if she might cry. "That seems so sad now, and I wish I could have handled it better. But that's what I did."

Patti was gone, the rest of us were with our father, and Mama was on her own. Ann Arbor was no longer home, and she had signed away the family car, the house, any claim to alimony, and custody of her four daughters.

Her mother had sent her a plane ticket, urging Mama to come to Garden Grove, California, which at first just made my mother mad. "Well! You think I'm going to go stay with mother, hah! I almost tore up the ticket."

But she was out of options. "I had some money to pay the rent, or feed me and buy my cigarettes, one or the other. I went out for a walk, and I thought about what I was going to do next, tomorrow, with my life, and I went and bought a suitcase. I spent the last of my money for a hotel room right next to the airport and took the next flight out to California."

She seemed very far away now, shaking her head slightly, staring straight ahead. Her voice was getting weaker.

Finally I asked, "Did you have any thoughts of coming to Washington?" It was almost as if I were back in 1962, bargaining, trying to help her find a solution that would have kept her closer, allowed us to at least see her sometimes.

She looked genuinely confused. "What?"

"I'm just wondering if that was even an option for you?"

She was honest, as always. "I don't remember even considering that." It had never crossed her mind. "I felt like I was loose on my own now and that was it. He had the kids, I was a failure at motherhood."

By this time we were all exhausted, and our mother suddenly remembered that she had medicine to take. I turned off the recorder,

THE GOOD POETIC MOTHER

we thanked her, and probably—certainly—hugged her. And left her alone.

The final poem in *Grandma Stories* was really the first chapter of the rest of our mother's life. Addressing the grandchild to whom her memoir was dedicated, the boy who never knew his poet grandfather but loved his grandma very much, it told the story of how our mother had written a letter to Bukowski, and he had called her up, and she had taken a bus and then a taxi into Los Angeles, hoping he'd keep his promise to pay the fare.

XXII – NEW LIFE
1963

He did keep his promise of course and she found out that Grandpa always kept his promises. He took her to the race track and the fights and drove her home to Garden Grove when the weekend was over. Now she had at last a poet friend and she was not quite so lonesome anymore. Grandpa and Grandma became lovers and that is how your beautiful blue-eyed mother was born and Poet Grandma began to trust her voice.

francEyE, Grandma Stories. *Conflux Press, 2008*

NOT UNTRUE AND NOT UNKIND
(CALIFORNIA, 2009)

As the jetliner began its final descent into Los Angeles, morning sun streamed into the cabin and I checked my itinerary one more time—rental car, map, directions up the Pacific Coast Highway to Santa Monica and the Cal Mar Hotel, where I was going to meet my family. It had been twenty-eight years since I made this trip the first time, hoping to find the mother I'd grown up without. Back then my son had been seven, and I'd been married to my second husband for two months.

The airport had expanded exponentially since the early eighties, and rental cars were no longer just steps away from the terminal. I had visited Los Angeles many times since that first visit—despite our failed first encounter, my mother and I ultimately formed a connection that was more than amicable, if not truly intimate—and I had made the trip even more often in recent months. Yet now I was struck, as I had been in 1981, by a sense of déjà vu so powerful that

THE GOOD POETIC MOTHER

I forgot for a moment where I was headed; I became overwhelmed with recognition, longing, and grief.

My second husband had been in the ground for a quarter century, the seven-year-old had sons of his own, and a daughter not dreamed of in 1981 had just finished college.

I had come for my mother's funeral.

I remembered the handsome two-story church at the corner of Second and Hill Streets, with its two-toned brick facade, sturdy bell tower, and terracotta tile roof. My mother's apartment had been a ten-minute walk from the Church in Ocean Park, where we had held my baby sister's memorial service five years earlier. I noticed a plaque commemorating the construction of the church in 1923, and realized that the building had been there almost exactly as long as my mother had been alive. The progressive interfaith congregation made few changes to their lovely old building, and the original stained-glass windows were still there. I am not much more attached to Christian stories and imagery than my Unitarian mother had been, but felt oddly comforted by the window depicting Jesus and his lambs under an olive tree and a sky as blue as the one over Ocean Park.

Patti would not be attending the service, and Ruthie, of course, was gone. But Sara was there, along with her family and mine, as well as our two half-sisters—Bukowski's daughter Marina, and our father's daughter, Anne.

I was not as numb as I had been at Ruthie's funeral, and was ready, I hoped, to stand up and say something about the part of my mother's life that her California friends never knew, the part she left out of her book. Someone read the poem that Bukowski wrote about my mother, calling her "Old Snaggletooth" with grudging fondness, telling of her eccentricities, how she liked solving puzzles and looked out for ants and plants. She had a hard life, he wrote, and perhaps he should have helped her more. I heard again the lines that had given me such difficulty when I first read them, "she has hurt fewer people than anybody I know, and if you look at it like that, well, she has created a better world."

And then it was my turn. I introduced myself—I'm from the East Coast, the second of our mother's first four daughters, a psychotherapist. I said I came from a family that one needs a degree in psychology to figure out, and people chuckled, gratefully. Some had no idea who I was, others did know, and perhaps feared what I might have come to say. I acknowledged Sara, Marina, and Anne, and realized in that moment that, after everything, there were again four sisters.

What I had come to say was that the woman many of them had known since 1963, the respected and prolific poet francEyE, had a life before she came to California. While her marriage was barely a decade and a half of her almost ninety years, it had been, until she left, my whole life. I reminded them of her memoir, *Grandma Stories*, published just a year earlier, and several people nodded and smiled. Faces turned somber as I told them, gently, that while her charming book included poems from her earliest infancy all the way to arriving in Los Angeles, where she met "the world's greatest poet," she left out all the years when she was married to our father and was our mother. What I had come to say was that those years mattered.

I told them of my initial reaction to being left out of my mother's book, and "this is what in the therapy business is called a narcissistic injury" got another laugh. I shared what I had only recently learned, that my mother had tried to write about those lost years, but had found herself unable to face them. In order to take on the second half

THE GOOD POETIC MOTHER

of her life, she had packed away both the good and the unbearable memories of the life she had left behind, and when she tried to open them up again, it brought on a despair so dangerous that she had to abandon the effort.

I described how francEyE referred to herself throughout her memoir—"Baby Grandma," "First-Grade Grandma," "Teen Grandma," and so on, and noted the two-decade gap between the penultimate poem, "Soldier Grandma" and the final piece, "Poet Grandma."

I told my mother's assembled fans and friends that I had decided to fill in what she couldn't bear to include. Imagining how she might have written the absent poems, I had added three more. "With all respect to the poet, I'd like to read these," I said. The fellowship hall was utterly silent, and I could feel my heart beating.

MISSING POEM #1
Soldier Grandma cracked codes during the war, and met another code-cracking soldier, a tall engineer who reminded her of her dead father. He wanted her but couldn't be happy with her and they never did crack that code.

MISSING POEM #2
The engineer and Mama Grandma had four little girls. Mama Grandma showed them how to make origami birds and bells, told them the names of wildflowers and constellations, taught them to swim and to take care of the natural world.

MISSING POEM #3
The engineer wanted an important life, a clean house, and to have everyone admire him. But Poet Grandma could never

keep house, didn't want that kind of life, and was tired of fighting. The engineer took their daughters, told them their mother was crazy and that they were better off without her. Everybody believed him, even Poet Grandma.

After the service, friends of our mother's came up to speak to me and my sisters, to hold my hand, tell me what francEyE meant to them. One said my mother had been "the grandmother I never had," and I saw my son wince. Another wanted me to know that "she really loved you all, you know," and I tried to believe that kind wish. "You're the therapist?" another asked. "She hated therapists, but always said you were one of the good ones."

A teenaged boy with curly red hair, wearing a T-shirt printed with a drawing of Bukowski waving a bottle, wanted to talk to me. "I've been reading Buk since I was ten," he said eagerly. "I didn't know your mom, but I always wished I could have met him!" Another fan, middle-aged, with a beard and a ball cap embroidered with the words *What Would Bukowski Do?* sidled up to us. I couldn't help laughing at the hat, and the man asked, "You knew Hank? Can I talk to you about him?"

When I told them I had never met the Great Poet, the Bukowski fans moved on.

We left the church in small groups, carrying with us the flowers that had decorated the podium, stage, and chairs. Stepping into the bright sunshine, I paused for a moment on the steps, looked back, and realized I was waiting for my mother to catch up with us.

The beach was four blocks away, down Ocean Park Boulevard to a shady park where paths curved across a lawn to the edge of the sand.

THE GOOD POETIC MOTHER

Just as I had done at my little sister's funeral, I took off my shoes and walked toward the water in stocking feet (I wasn't sure anyone else was wearing stockings this time, either). A mile north, through a gathering haze, the Ferris wheel towered above the Santa Monica Pier, where my mother once worked, sometime during the years when I didn't know where she was.

The others stood back, waiting for the daughters to go first, and at the water's edge we tossed our bouquets into the Pacific. The waves sent mine back to the sand, and I had to retrieve the sodden blossoms and throw them out again with more determination and a stronger arm.

I had dreams about my mother all through the final weeks of her life. In one dream she invites me to a fundraiser for a "very important cause," suggests I "buy a bunch of tables." I can't do that, know I've disappointed her, and wonder if I'm a bad daughter after all. In another dream, she wants me to sing "Amazing Grace" at her funeral. I can't find the music, search frantically for a songbook, and forget until I wake up that I know that song by heart, just as I do the song whose name she gave me. Like her, the dreams were not easy to understand, but I was glad to see her.

The best dream, not long after her death, was about a writing workshop (I like workshops, like my mother did, and Bukowski didn't) where I'm talking about my almost-finished book. I explain that my mother left when I was a teenager, lived with that now-famous outsider poet, that I never met him, but did manage to establish a relationship with her, by the end. I turn to the woman on my right and see a long white braid, hazel eyes behind large glasses, and a ball cap with *Snaggletooth*, or maybe *francEyE*, embroidered on it.

NOT UNTRUE AND NOT UNKIND (CALIFORNIA, 2009)

I'm telling my fellow writers how grateful I'd been to attend her funeral, to have been able to find words that were, as another poet said, *not untrue and not unkind.* I turn again to the woman I recognize as my mother, confused—she's right there, but she can't be, because she's dead. Still, she's listening, she does not disagree, and—as her fellow poets remember her at readings—she's nodding and smiling.

She caused me to weep, she caused me to moan
She caused me to leave my home
And the very last words I ever heard her say,
was, please sing me one more song.
Goodnight Irene, goodnight Irene
I'll see you in my dreams.

ACKNOWLEDGMENTS

I must begin with immense gratitude to the New Directions writing program of the Washington Baltimore Center for Psychoanalysis, especially my fellow alumni writing group members Devra Adelstein, Sharon Bisco, Mary Cummins, John Gualtieri, and Elizabeth Trawick, as well as our leaders Deirdre Callanan and Joannie Lieberman.

I had the good fortune to be a participant in Sara Taber's "Twilight Memoir Club," where, over the course of five rewarding years, I workshopped almost every piece of what would become this memoir. Sara gave me the confidence to discover the Kenyon Review Summer Writers Workshop, where I learned from instructors Rebecca McClanahan, Dinty W. Moore, David H. Lynn, and E.J. Levy, and met dear friends Larry I. Palmer, Kelly Fig Smith, Allison K. Williams, and too many others to count. The Blue Flower Arts Winter Writing Workshop brought me the wonderful poet and teacher Mark Doty, and Bryan Monte, the editor who would bring into being my very first publication. At the Vermont College of Fine Arts Postgraduate Conference, I worked with Sue William Silverman and benefited from the warm and generous input of fellow students, many of whom remain friends.

Thanks also to the Third Sunday Writers, Joyce Dehli, Martha Young Freedberg, and Kaja Weeks.

Diane Zinna earns most special gratitude, both for the AWP Writer-to-Writer mentorship program she founded, where I was matched in 2016 with an experienced and generous mentor Claude Clayton (Bud) Smith, and for her wise and warm friendship since. Bud was the first of four developmental editors, followed by Sarah Einstein, Sue William Silverman, and Dinty W. Moore, all of whom helped make this book better.

I also thank *Amsterdam Quarterly*, *Vine Leaves Literary Journal*, *Stonecoast Review*, *Wisconsin Review*, and *Delmarva Review*, publishers of essays that made their way in various forms into this book.

PERMISSIONS

"One for Old Snaggle-Tooth"
in *Love is a Dog From Hell* by Charles Bukowski. © Copyright 1977 by Charles Bukowski. Used by permission of HarperCollins Publishers.

"Goodnight, Irene"
Words and Music by Huddie Ledbetter and John A. Lomax
TRO - © Copyright 1936 (Renewed) 1950 (Renewed) Ludlow Music, Inc., New York, NY
Used by Permission.

The following works are used by permission of the estate of Frances Dean Smith (francEyE):

"Autobiography"
 by Frances Dean Smith, 1962. Unpublished.

"Nursery, 1963"
by Frances Dean Smith, 1963. Unpublished.

"Keeping House III"
in *Sciamachy* Vol. 6, 1964 by S. S. Veri (Frances Dean Smith).

"May 19" by francEyE, 2000. Unpublished.

"COUNTING" by francEyE, 2004. Unpublished.

"XXII—NEW LIFE *1963* Garden Grove and Los Angeles, California.
in *Grandma Stories* by francEyE. Conflux Press. © Copyright 2008 by francEyE.

"Call"
in *CALL* by francEyE, edited by S. A. Griffin. Rose of Sharon Press. © Copyright 2008 by francEyE.

www.ingramcontent.com/pod-product-compliance
Lightning Source LLC
Chambersburg PA
CBHW072001110526
44592CB00012B/1164